CURIOUS LEARNERS in PRIMARY MATHS, SCIENCE, COMPUTING and DT

SAGE was founded in 1965 by Sara Miller McCune to support the dissemination of usable knowledge by publishing innovative and high-quality research and teaching content. Today, we publish over 900 journals, including those of more than 400 learned societies, more than 800 new books per year, and a growing range of library products including archives, data, case studies, reports, and video. SAGE remains majority-owned by our founder, and after Sara's lifetime will become owned by a charitable trust that secures our continued independence.

Los Angeles | London | New Delhi | Singapore | Washington DC | Melbourne

CURIOUS LEARNERS in PRIMARY MATHS, SCIENCE, COMPUTING and DT

Alan Cross, Alison Borthwick, Karen Beswick, Jon Board AND Jon Chippindall

Los Angeles | London | New Delhi
Singapore | Washington DC | Melbourne

Los Angeles | London | New Delhi
Singapore | Washington DC | Melbourne

SAGE Publications Ltd
1 Oliver's Yard
55 City Road
London EC1Y 1SP

SAGE Publications Inc.
2455 Teller Road
Thousand Oaks, California 91320

SAGE Publications India Pvt Ltd
B 1/I 1 Mohan Cooperative Industrial Area
Mathura Road
New Delhi 110 044

SAGE Publications Asia-Pacific Pte Ltd
3 Church Street
#10-04 Samsung Hub
Singapore 049483

Editor: Amy Thornton
Production Editor: Chris Marke
Marketing Manager: Lorna Patkai
Cover Design: Wendy Scott
Typeset by: C&M Digitals (P) Ltd, Chennai, India
Printed and bound by CPI Group (UK) Ltd,
Croydon, CR0 4YY

Library of Congress Control Number: 2016940060

British Library Cataloguing in Publication Data

A catalogue record for this book is available from the British Library.

ISBN: 978-1-4739-5238-6
ISBN: 978-1-4739-5237-9 (hbk)

At SAGE we take sustainability seriously. Most of our products are printed in the UK using FSC papers and boards. When we print overseas we ensure sustainable papers are used as measured by the PREPS grading system. We undertake an annual audit to monitor our sustainability.

CONTENTS

ACKNOWLEDGEMENTS

The authors would like to thank the pupils and staff of the following schools:

Chapel Break Infant School, Norfolk

Cringleford Primary School, Norfolk

Crumpsall Lane Primary School, Manchester

Hevingham Primary School, Norfolk

Lionwood Junior School, Norfol

Mauldeth Road Primary School, Manchester

Wesley Methodist Primary School, Bury

West Earlham Junior School, Norfolk

Thanks for her valuable assistance – Charlotte Morton.

Thanks for the photograph of Alan Turing's statue – Tim Chippindall.

ABOUT THE AUTHORS

Alan Cross

Alan teaches primary science, DT and Computing at the University of Manchester as well providing CPD in primary science and DT and writing about science for primary students and teachers. Alan has published in refereed journals and has recently co-authored *Essential Primary* Science (2nd edition), OU Press with Adrian Bowden and also in 2014 *Creative Ways to Teach Primary Science,* OU Press with Jon Board. Alan is a school governor, has worked as an Ofsted inspector of schools and HEI, external examiner and has contributed to primary science projects around the world.

Alison Borthwick

Alison has over 20 years' experience as a teacher, local authority adviser, governor, Ofsted inspector and freelance consultant. She has also worked in ITT for several institutions supporting mathematics courses and has been involved in several international projects for mathematics. Alison has researched and published material on children's calculations strategies and children's perceptions of, and attitudes towards, mathematics lessons.

Karen Beswick

Karen has 20 years' experience teaching in the primary, secondary and tertiary sectors. She has worked as an Advanced Skills Teacher and local authority advisor, providing tailored programmes for schools and whole borough CPD in science. Karen is the Primary Science National Lead and University tutor for *Teach*

First, a governor, and provides CPD for primary curriculum leads. She teaches science, design technology, cross-curricular and early years at The University of Manchester.

Jon Board

Jon teaches science at Mauldeth Road Primary School and contributes to the PGCE Primary Science course at The University of Manchester. He has a particular interest in encouraging the scientific enquiry skill of questioning and in developing effective models for understanding in primary science. Jon has published in the area of primary science including co-authoring *Creative Ways to Teach Primary Science* (2014) OU Press and the international science scheme of work – Cambridge Primary Science. He has worked abroad, training primary teachers in countries such as Egypt, Mongolia and the Middle East.

Jon Chippindall

Jon has taught for five years and is currently the Computing Coordinator at Crumpsall Lane Primary School, Manchester, where he specialises in teaching Computing. He is a CAS Master Teacher and runs the popular computing blog www.primary computing.co.uk. He helped develop the DfE Barefoot Computing resources and delivers computing CPD with schools nationally.

ABOUT THIS BOOK

Curiosity has the potential to enhance learning in all curriculum subjects. This book is about curiosity and how it impacts on four primary school subjects, which can be grouped under the abbreviation of STEM; these are science, technology, engineering and mathematics (see www.stem.org.uk). In this book we have chosen to include science, mathematics, computing and design and technology. These four subjects all rely very heavily on qualitative values or numbers. Of course, curiosity manifests itself in all subjects, for example, in the study of English, English literature, the arts and the humanities. Sadly, we don't, in this book, have space for all primary subjects. This book considers the teaching for learning of our identified four Primary STEM subjects, which like all subjects require a degree of curiosity. Or perhaps it is better to say that these subjects benefit from learners and teachers who display curiosity?

Structure of the book

Following the introduction, the book is divided into pairs of chapters in which the first chapter sets out the meaning of curiosity in the particular subject and how the subject can enhance a learner's curiosity. The authors consider examples of individuals, who through their curiosity have been leaders in their field. They include references to the National Curriculum (DfE, 2013). They will refer to relevant literature including Ofsted and other reports. The second chapter will then draw on case study and other exemplary material, which will mean that by the end of each pair of chapters readers will:

- understand the relevance of curiosity to that subject;
- know which aspects of the subject are most influenced by curiosity;

- see how curiosity in teachers can enable curiosity in learners in the subject;
- appreciate a wide range of ways to develop curiosity through examples given.

The introductory chapter reviews the thinking of writers and researchers who have considered curiosity in people and younger learners. Chapters on mathematics, science, design and technology and computing then follow.

STEM link to mathematics

In the mathematics chapters we will see how curiosity is linked to mathematics in terms of content, aims (fluency, problem solving, reasoning), skills and the attributes of mathematical thinkers (DfE, 2013). It will show that at its very heart mathematics itself is curious about number, proportionality, geometry, etc. This chapter will refer to the beauty and romance of mathematics through approaches such as a mathematically curious classroom. It will also consider how Stephen Hawking exploited curiosity to seek answers to some of the most complex questions in the universe.

STEM link to science

In science, curiosity is seen as the key driver which leads to scientific questions and in some cases profound questions and answers. It will refer to the National Curriculum (DfE, 2013) and the place of curiosity within 'Working Scientifically' and in relation to science ideas and phenomena in the world. It will provide examples and draw from evidence including Ofsted's *Maintaining Curiosity* (2013) and consider the degrees of curiosity which might be observed in different children. The chapter will use Mary Anning as an example of a person who was curious about the interestingly shaped rocks she found on the beach.

STEM link to computing

Computing is the newest subject to the curriculum (DfE, 2013). Computing will be presented as a medium/world for exploration through programming or coding, debugging and computer networks. It will include simple approaches such as exploring algorithms in 'computing unplugged' through to more complex programming with a range of languages such as Scratch Junior, Scratch, Python, Logo, etc. There will be clear reference to tinkering with code, debugging and how internet searches occur.

STEM link to design and technology

Curiosity about design and technology is about curiosity in the man-made world of artefacts where children confidently build and display curious behaviours (e.g. exploring the strength of materials, observing how doings work, how things are made/assembled). It will link to the National Curriculum (DfE, 2013) and to ideas about design and technology. It will consider lessons for the psychology of learning (e.g. schema, when do children start to display this behaviour?) and link to Kimbell et al.'s (1991) interaction of hand and mind in design and technology. It will consider aesthetics and the different responses of individuals to problems and design briefs.

The final chapter of this book will consider how the four (primary) STEM subjects can be used in an integrated and immersive way, and offers a different pedagogical style of teaching and learning which fuels curiosity and curious learners.

CHAPTER 1

INTRODUCTION

I HAVE NO SPECIAL TALENTS. I AM ONLY PASSIONATELY CURIOUS.

ALBERT EINSTEIN

Chapter objectives

After reading this chapter you will:

- have a strongly developing understanding of the term curiosity;
- appreciate the value of curiosity to primary education through the four STEM subjects;
- be curious about the rest of the book.

What is curiosity?

Curiosity is observed in human beings wherever we observe people engaging with the world around them or with their personal thoughts. They play, explore and reflect in ways that move their ideas forward. We display, as a species, a natural curiosity about the world around us and the world of our thoughts. We may be the most curious beings in the Universe. Our society values curiosity highly. Being curious encourages progress, innovation and creativity. Curiosity has led to the biggest ideas and innovations in science, mathematics, computing and design and technology.

Our young appear to be born curious, a capacity we value in them as they explore the world they discover. Young children quickly begin to observe and question the behaviour of others, wonder about the objects in the night sky and even become curious about their own thoughts and feelings, including their own acquisition of knowledge. Parents often have to warn children about dangers they may encounter as their curiosity drives them to explore and investigate, for example, living things, fire, water, falling objects and more.

> *Two-year-old Amy stared intently at the brightly coloured insect: What was it? Did it fly? Would it make a noise? Could it be a pet? She carefully reached out to pick it up and felt her first sharp burning sting from a wasp (Vespula vulgaris). Curiosity is a powerful but sometimes heartless teacher.*

Loewenstein (1994) recognised that there are a number of information-seeking behaviours, but that curiosity is important as it results in such a wide range of information seeking. Loewenstein and others (e.g. Litman, 2005; Dewey, 1910; Berlyne, 1954) have considered curiosity from a number of perspectives. There are different views about curiosity, its cause, its nature, its determinants and manifestations. As teachers it is important to know that curiosity is powerful, is not fully understood or explained but that attempts, including research, to understand it gives us useful insights which can influence our teaching and learning.

CASE STUDY

Dancing robots

STEM link to design and technology

Year 5 learners tackling a cross-curricular STEM project attempt to make a programmable dancing robot. In this example it is curiosity which drove pupils to tinker with materials and different methods of construction, wondering to themselves about the best way of assembling components and asking questions such as 'Would it be better this way than that? Let's try'.

As the electronics are fitted learners quickly add the battery, curious to see if the motor will turn (some pupils are led 'off-task' by their curiosity as they notice a small group fiddling with a battery and bulb determined to get the bulb to illuminate). When pupils start programming, they look expectantly at the robot for signs of an output, some movement. When nothing happens they try reordering the code, curious to know why it isn't working. More questions follow, some aimed at the

STEM link to computing

Figure 1.1 Electronic buggy

teacher, some at others in the group, all with the same intention: to further their understanding so they can get the robot dancing. It is their curiosity which is driving this pursuit of knowledge; they want to see what this robot can do! As questioning, exploring and perseverance leads them to crack the basics of coding, their curiosity turns to their knowledge of mathematics. What percentage power do we need? What ratio of power to the left and right wheels will make the robot turn? Can we get it to turn through 360°?

STEM link to mathematics

Finally, during the robot dance-off that concludes the project, pupils' focus of curiosity shifts to their peers. What have they managed to get their robot to do? Will it be 'better' than ours? How did you get it to do that? What else can the robot do?

This example shows that schools can and should be considered hotbeds for curiosity. Curiosity should not be confined to the children but to all learners and adults seeking knowledge, understanding and greater skill. For teachers this includes professional curiosity and the objective of harnessing learners' natural curiosity. As we move into the twenty-first century employers are looking for people who can do more than follow rules and procedures (Royal Society, 2014). The world needs people who have an intrinsic desire to learn, to advance, to solve problems and to question. But it is not always the easy path. So, our schools need to become places that cultivate curiosity and curious leaners.

Curious about curiosity?

As adults, we feel our curiosity aroused on most days. For example, 'shocking' newspaper headlines entice us to read more, we refresh social media to feed our curiosity about other people's lives, we have hobbies and interests driven by our curiosity to learn more, and we seek out films and books to purposefully evoke a feeling of curiosity.

Curiosity can, of course, be a positive thing but, as the saying goes, curiosity killed the cat. Curiosity can be negative; for example, curiosity about recreational drugs, other dangerous or illegal activities or an unhealthy interest in the lives of others. Curiosity also makes us ask big questions of ourselves and our existence. Indeed, it is our capacity to wonder and desire to know which drives human exploration. When peering up at the stars in the night sky, for example, it is hard not to feel a sense of curiosity. Where did it all come from? Does it ever end? Is there life out there?

Helping to answer some of these big questions, NASA's Curiosity rover blasted off from Cape Canaveral on 26 November 2011 destined for the planet Mars. Over the next ten months it made the 350-million mile journey to its landing site, Gale Crater, where it touched down and started returning remarkable images of the landscape (Figure 1.2) as well as undertaking investigations into the planet's make up. Negating the near 300 tons of kerosene and oxidizer in the launch vehicle, the fuel for Curiosity's mission was the collective inquisitiveness of NASA's scientists and engineers, curiosity itself.

So, what actually is curiosity? Where does it come from? Are there different types of curiosity? Is the desire to explore the surface of Mars the same as the desire to know the latest celebrity gossip? Are some people more curious than others; if true, is that a good or a bad thing? Can we teach pupils to be curious? Can curiosity be killed? How should curiosity be harnessed in primary education? Is this curiosity about curiosity?

STEM link to science

STEM link to mathematics

Figure 1.2 Martian landscape from Curiosity rover (https://commons.wikimedia.org/wiki/Category:Curiosity_rover#/media/File:Mars-2015.jpg)

Reflective activity

Take a moment to reflect on what makes you curious. This might be a short-lived interest, something which caught your attention, as you were curious to find out more. Or a more long-term set of interests and hobbies you have. What do you enjoy reading about, for example?

Keep your own curiosities in mind as we explore four models of curiosity. Which do you feel best describes your own experience of being curious?

First model: Is curiosity a drive?

Throughout the 1960s many psychologists sought to explain the cause of curiosity and a popular theory at the time was to consider curiosity as an innate 'drive'. Drive theory was developed by, among others, Sigmund Freud (2015), who said we are born with innate drives such as hunger, thirst and sex. While there was deliberation as to whether curiosity could be added to this primary list, or whether it was a secondary drive, many researchers agreed that the exploratory and explanation-seeking behaviour of humans was to satisfy an innate curiosity drive.

This certainly appears true when we consider the behaviour of babies and young children, who bristle with curiosity about the world around them. From a very young age babies point and babble at objects as they look to others for help in explaining the world they inhabit. It is also the same curiosity we blame when young children end up with fingers stuck in small holes or half a flower hanging out of their mouth.

 Reflective activity

Take a moment to think about the behaviours of pupils in your school. How many of their behaviours appear to be an outward display of an internal innate curiosity? What behaviours are these? Do we see these more in Early Years settings? How are classrooms arranged to encourage this behaviour? Do classrooms discourage this behaviour?

Second model: Is curiosity the result of 'violated expectations'?

This model was developed by a different set of researchers, including the Swiss developmental psychologist Jean Piaget (1958). Here, it is said, that our curiosity is evoked when an incongruity is experienced between what someone expects and what happens, i.e. when we are surprised. This model appears to explain the curiosity we might feel at 'shocking' newspaper headlines we don't expect to read. It may also explain why children are so curious so much of the time, as working on the simple models they hold about the world around them, everything appears to violate their expectations and so demands explanation.

This theory also suggests that this type of curiosity has positive emotions attached to it. Presenting curiosity as a pleasurable feeling may explain why we seek out stimuli that make us curious.

 Activity

Can you relate this model to your own experience of being curious? What has recently caught your attention and made you curious? Did this violate your expectations of something? Can you relate to the sense of anxiety described above? Perhaps you have started learning something new and felt 'overwhelmed' by the information to take in? This might be the case if you have just started your teacher training!

Third model: Curiosity – a matter of a reference point?

In 1994 George Loewenstein published a seminal paper on curiosity (Loewenstein, 1994). The paper was in two parts; the first reviewed much of the work on curiosity from the 1960s, and the second presented a new model: the idea that curiosity was a reference point phenomenon. Loewenstein explains that curiosity is a response to an information gap, the difference between what we know and what we want to know. Put simply, curiosity is sparked when we become aware of what we don't know. Importantly, he proposed that it is the process of closing this gap which is pleasurable, explaining why people seek to satisfy their curiosities.

Viewing curiosity in this way leads to some interesting implications. First, it is unlikely that we can be curious about something we are completely ignorant of. Conversely, we are likely to be less curious about something we perceive to know everything about. Unless you are aware of the information gap, it is difficult to get interested in the subject matter and this has implications for the ways we might teach, as will be explored later in this book.

Fourth model: To seek *and* satisfy?

The fourth and final model of curiosity we will consider was proposed by Jordan Litman (2005). Litman sought to reconcile the contrasting views listed above which present curiosity as either an aversive mechanism to satisfy (drive theory) or a pleasurable mechanism we pursue (incongruence and reference point). In short, Litman suggested it could be a bit of both, giving the example of when our hunger may arouse from internal nutritional deficits, or from the sight of a good-looking chocolate cake. In either case, the act of eating the cake is pleasurable, whether we chose to eat it because we needed a sugar fix or just because it looked appealing. We may feel either curious and/or motivated to learn to fill a knowledge gap and/or simply for the pleasure of learning something new.

 Reflective activity

Take a moment to reflect on how your own experience of being curious sits with the four models discussed above. Does one model feel like it better explains your own experiences, or can you relate to parts of each? Maybe your different curiosities feel/are different? Is the desire to learn more about the art of teaching driven by a different mechanism than the craving to know what you're missing on Twitter?

We acknowledge that there are other types of curiosity that we simply do not have time to discuss in this book. However, we hope we have given you a flavour of the different ways that curiosity can appear and be evoked. Figure 1.3 summarises ideas about curiosity in learners relevant to this book.

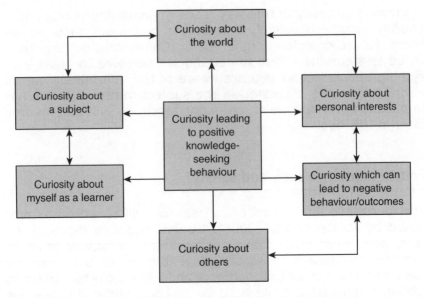

Figure 1.3 Layers of curiosity

As we have shown above a number of definitions of curiosity exist, but we have adopted Litman's (2005) definition as we feel it is a useful basis for teachers considering curiosity in the classroom. Litman said curiosity is 'a desire to know, to see, or to experience that motivates exploratory behaviour directed towards the acquisition of new information'.

The opportunity to develop curiosity would be considerably enhanced by the presence of a growth mindset. For many years now researchers (e.g. Dweck, 2006) have collected data, which shows that everyone has a core belief about how they learn. Some people believe that they are born with a fixed level of intelligence, which despite acknowledging the power to learn things, ultimately results in your basic level of intelligence being unaltered. This is known as having a fixed mindset. However, there are also people who believe that this level of intelligence can increase with hard work. This is known as a growth mindset.

Our mindset is incredibly important as it sets out and controls our learning behaviours. Positive, curious learning behaviours can lead to learners achieving higher levels in their education. Often, people with fixed mindsets have negative views of aspects of their educational lives. Too often this fixed mindset can have devastating effects on learners who believe they are no good at certain subjects, despite the amount of effort they put in. The good news is that we can change our mindset.

Dweck (2006) and Boaler (2016) emphasise the need for educators and learners to see the brain as a muscle which can grow. The capacity of the brain is, they might say, only limited by a frame of mind, which sees limits to our learning. There are many aspects to achieving a growth mindset, but interestingly one of the characteristics is that errors and mistakes are viewed as positive things. They talk of mistakes as part of brain exercise, allowing your brain to spark and grow. This evidence is rooted in scientific studies by Moser et al. (2011), who have studied the neural mechanisms that operate in our brains. They discovered that there are two potential responses when we make a mistake. The first occurs when our brain recognises that there is conflict between a correct response and a mistake. This response occurs whether we are conscious of the mistake or not. The second response is a brain signal that consciously reflects the mistake. So, even if we are aware of making a mistake or not, our brain has sparked and when it does, it grows.

As teachers we can encourage learners to develop a growth mindset. We can change the way learners view mistakes; we can show them that within any subject it is the skills and knowledge we apply and use, rather than the amount of facts they can remember; we can give learners rich tasks that encourage them to think, persevere, struggle and use different starting points; we can show them that they can all access the same task at their own level; and finally we can believe in all learners and praise their effort in tasks. This could be a checklist for capturing curiosity.

Today's context

One overarching aim of the English National Curriculum (DfE, 2013) is to organise the content and knowledge offered to pupils and to help 'engender an appreciation of human creativity and achievement'. One way to scaffold a curriculum is to exploit a link between subjects (e.g. Barnes, 2011; Rose, 2009; Alexander, 2010). Primary STEM offers a coherent link between subjects grounded in a world where quantitative values contribute very strongly. The advent of STEAM (science, technology, engineering, arts and mathematics) recognises the undoubted value of other subjects. Subject links like these have been seen in curricula around the world, such as STS (Science and Technology in Society) (Solomon, 1993).

Mathematics is full of surprises! Just when you think you have grasped a concept (e.g. all shapes tessellate) the outcome changes (circles do not tessellate) and you have to think again. Helping children to make sense of the world mathematically relies on cultivating and nurturing this curiosity. Whether we love or hate mathematics, we are still curious about it. We are curious if our numbers will come up on the National Lottery, or if the temperature will be hot enough tomorrow for a visit to the beach or whether we are getting the best two-for-one deal in the supermarket. However, while some people are aware of the mathematical connections invading their everyday lives, others are not. The purpose of the latest mathematics curriculum (DfE, 2013) is to encourage 'a sense of enjoyment and curiosity about the subject'. This link between enjoyment and curiosity is important and one that the mathematics chapters in this book will explore further.

The National Curriculum (DfE, 2013) reminds us that high-quality science education encourages 'a sense of excitement and curiosity about natural phenomena' in pupils who will be inspired to satisfy their curiosity by asking questions about their observations. Most people recognise that scientists tend to be curious and that science education can harness and strengthen natural curiosity in learners.

With computing, a new subject now established within the latest National Curriculum (DfE, 2013), we might say it is a subject born of curiosity. Ever since the first mechanical computing engines (Swade, 2001) and their automation and the invention of Random Access Memory there has been a quest to miniaturise and make these machines ever more powerful.

Design and technology is a subject about human-made artefacts. These artefacts are all around in our man-made world, each fulfilling a perceived human need (e.g. a pull-along toy for a two-year-old). The designer of children's toys would be curious about which function, shape, colour, etc. will appeal to the child. He or she will need to research the interests and motivations of these young children, perhaps even testing colour preferences, trialling prototypes, scoring different reactions and moving to carefully drawn plans including measures, shape and proportions.

This call for teachers to encourage curiosity extends to the English Teacher Standards (DfE, 2013) – 4b 'promote a love of learning and intellectual curiosity' (DfE, 2012). Dunn (2013) points out that teachers may not be well prepared to develop curiosity. This cuts to the heart of the need for this book and its aim to clarify approaches to curiosity in mathematics, science, computing and design and technology.

The four subjects dealt with by this book are perhaps subjects not readily associated by everyone with curiosity but which, like all subjects, benefit from what Cicero called a 'passion for learning' (Loewenstein, 1994). What was it that drove Curie to shovel and crush tons of pitchblende in her search of tiny quantities of radium, which ultimately ruined her health (Quinn, 1995)? Why

STEM link
to
mathematics

STEM link
to science

did Pythagoras spend time considering the relationship between the squares of the sides of triangles? Why did Dyson completely review the design of the vacuum cleaner? The lure of financial profit or academic prowess might also be a motivation but a simple desire to know almost always precedes more tangible benefits. STEM subjects, like others, can be about so-called blue-sky thinking – that is, thinking without any obvious application. We should not be embarrassed to say that curiosity is often driven by some profit motive or other. Graphene (thin layers of pure carbon that could be used in the future to revolutionise computing, smoke detectors, etc.), discovered in Manchester in 2004 will make millions of dollars for businesses around the world. Its applications in technology and medicine will ultimately benefit millions of people. But it was discovered by the human curious desire to know more.

STEM subjects and the associated developments and discoveries tend to be much sought after by nations and corporations. It is important that STEM subjects link to and learn from other primary school subjects but also that they are not seen as dry dusty subjects where learners simply hear about the discoveries of earlier pioneers in the field. Learners need to feel part of the story of the subject, that the subject is relevant to them and their lives, and that they can engage as young mathematicians, scientists, coders and designers.

The subject knowledge around these STEM subjects can challenge teachers. Few primary teachers would at the point of initial training see themselves as expert in all four subjects. This book's focus on curiosity will help, but we would recommend other books to enable you to strengthen subject knowledge in each subject as you require: for science, see Cross and Bowden (2014); for mathematics, Haylock (2010); for computing, Berry (2013a; 2013b) and materials at http://barefootcas.org.uk or http://primary.quickstartcomputing.org and for design and technology, Newton (2005).

Curiosity and knowledge

Curiosity about our own learning is part of metacognition (Flavell, 1979). Metacognition is not a word used in primary classrooms, or rarely in staff rooms, but teachers use metacognition every day. Knowing about knowing, or metacognition, is that area which accepts that we are conscious beings and have an inner life. Everything we learn is processed internally. We have all said to ourselves at some point, 'yes, now I understand that' having struggled with an idea. As teachers we are even more interested in knowing about knowing because we are in the knowing business and experienced teachers can all point to instances of having

STEM link to mathematics

taught things. Sometimes teaching is straightforward and some-times it is more challenging. Teachers, not surprisingly, love strate-gies and knowledge which allow them to teach more things more effectively to more learners. It is our strong view that curiosity is part of that teacher knowledge. Learners' curiosity is therefore a big idea, which can powerfully influence learning. Finding those ways which spark and maintain learner curiosity will focus learners' attention on what should be very carefully planned sets of experi-ence in lessons which harness that attention and drive learning.

Conclusion

Mathematics, science, computing and design and technology can be huge fun to teach and to learn but can present challenges to teachers and learners. Successful learners are resilient. When they encounter difficulty they are not ambushed, they under-stand challenge and respond with determination. As well as a spark that can initiate enquiry, curiosity can also strengthen a person's determination to develop an idea or enquiry. Curiosity might be part of the drive that helps maintain a focus that demands a full explanation or clarifies how an enquiry might be further pursued in search of knowledge.

Primary teachers are in a particularly powerful position to stim-ulate or encourage curiosity through the learning contexts they develop and the ways they scaffold learning with challenges, expla-nations and invitations to think and act. We teach learners in their formative years – they will then remember our actions and words for years if we model and encourage curiosity, value it and reward it; we could be empowering learners for a lifetime! Curiosity does not lie in government documents, it exists in human minds and is manifested in thinking and behaving curiously. This book is about curiosity in primary school, exemplified in four subjects.

Chapter summary

Having read the chapter you will:

- be clear about what we mean by curiosity;
- be able to refer to some of the theoretical writing about curiosity;
- understand that curiosity has considerable value to learners and the learning of each STEM subject.

CHAPTER 2

CURIOUS LEARNERS IN PRIMARY MATHEMATICS

A TEACHER OF MATHEMATICS HAS A GREAT OPPORTUNITY. IF HE FILLS HIS ALLOTTED TIME WITH DRILLING HIS STUDENTS IN ROUTINE OPERATIONS HE KILLS THEIR INTEREST, HAMPERS THEIR INTELLECTUAL DEVELOPMENT, AND MISUSES HIS OPPORTUNITY. BUT IF HE CHALLENGES THE CURIOSITY OF HIS STUDENTS BY SETTING THEM PROBLEMS PROPORTIONATE TO THEIR KNOWLEDGE, AND HELPS THEM TO SOLVE THEIR PROBLEMS WITH STIMULATING QUESTIONS, HE MAY GIVE THEM A TASTE FOR, AND SOME MEANS OF, INDEPENDENT THINKING.

POLYA, 1945

Chapter objectives

After reading this chapter you will:

- be curious about how mathematics can be used to enhance curiosity;
- be able to identify opportunities in mathematics that enable curiosity to be sparked and developed;
- have a strongly developing understanding of how curiosity impacts on the learning of mathematics.

Overview

Fostering curiosity in mathematics is more than simply acquiring facts and knowledge. While these are important and essential parts of mathematics, Polya (1945) rightly suggested that independent thinking is an essential quality to have. Curiosity in mathematics is driven by the value of questions and a confidence to pose questions, reason about numbers and data, and pursue an interest in new knowledge and understanding.

The English mathematics curriculum (DfE, 2013) is made up of two components: the objectives set out for each year group representing the mathematics content and the three aims of the mathematics curriculum, found in the introduction, fluency, reasoning and problem solving (DfE, 2013). These aims represent the 'using and applying' strand that has been the key ingredient of previous incarnations of the English mathematics curriculum, previously framed in terms such as problem solving or investigations. They encapsulate the important applicability of mathematics to the real world. It is, after all, the point of pupils learning schools mathematics, so that they can use and apply it out of the school context. But where does curiosity fit in?

Curiosity is an underpinning attitude, which is a prerequisite for active engagement with the mathematical world through reasoning and problem solving with increasing fluency. The mathematical aims direct learners to investigate, ask questions and be curious about the mathematics they are exploring. Fluency, according to Russell (2000), has three elements to it: efficiency, accuracy and flexibility. It is more than learning a single procedure or finding just one answer to a problem. For many learners the discovery that mathematics is not always black and white with only one answer can itself spark curiosity towards what other possible answers might be discovered. Suddenly mathematics is not limited to finding the correct answer, but perhaps it is about searching for a pattern, making a conjecture or testing out a theory. Reasoning supports learners' ability to use mathematics fluently by demanding an explanation, a reason or simply some initial thoughts. Finally, problem solving is the ultimate challenge in mathematics. It employs the previous two aims in an attempt to follow a line of enquiry to solving the problem presented.

But we can also find opportunities to create curiosity within the content section too. This section underlines the current (DfE, 2013) age-related expectations for learners under familiar headings such as place value, number, geometry and statistics. Each different part of mathematics has the opportunity to offer learners opportunities to be curious. Presented in the right way, who isn't curious about which numbers are happy or sad, as well as odd or even? Geometry too is a fascinating area to explore and be curious about. All learners have already begun to think geometrically, even before they go to school, as they try to build towers with wooden blocks or fit the cylinder shape into the cube space.

In one way mathematics is at the heart of curiosity within this book, as the following chapters will show that much of the learning and curiosity around science, computing, design and technology all involve mathematics. It may be the last initial within STEM but it is woven through all STEM subjects. Just as Senechal (1990) believes that 'the study of shape draws on and contributes to not only mathematics but also the science and the arts', mathematics is part of the other three subjects in this book, and the reason why mathematics precedes the other chapters.

A mathematician

There are many mathematicians who might feature within this section. The multidiscipline of the STEM context encourages us to consider curious individuals who employ skills, knowledge and understanding from different disciplines. Professor Stephen Hawking has a thirst for understanding that compelled him to defy his elders, colleagues and even doctors who gave him two years to live at the age of twenty-one. He is one of the most influential thinkers of our time and probably associated more with science than mathematics. However, as this book will show, the STEM subjects are very closely related and often trade in one another's domain. When asked, Professor Hawking has replied that as an astronomer, he has spent his life looking for a single theory that describes our Universe and how we may predict black holes. As a student he says he was drawn to both science and mathematics and it is these two subjects, which work in tandem to support and extend one another, that allows Hawking to continue his scientific work. Without mathematics, science would lack meaning and pattern.

Hawking's life and work perfectly illustrate the theme of this book as he often explores concepts that would seem better suited to fiction rather than fact. His curiosity feeds us as we observe his work. For example, in his book *The Universe in a Nutshell* (2001) Chapter 6 begins with a reference (and a screen shot) to the television and film world of *Star Trek* (*Star Trek: The Next Generation*, 2001, Paramount Pictures). Even if you are not interested in either *Star Trek* or Stephen Hawking, you could not help but to be slightly curious about this unlikely combination.

STEM link to science

Figure 2.1   Professor Stephen Hawking in NASA's zero gravity flight

People's perceptions and attitudes towards mathematics and mathematicians vary and for some can be negative, perhaps influenced by social or school experiences (Borthwick, 2008). This does not help to promote the curiosity that mathematics can offer. Professor Stephen Hawking is different. He is well known for his sharp wit and more recently has even become an icon of popular culture, making guest appearances on television shows like *The Simpsons* or lending his distinctive voice to Pink Floyd's album *The Division Bell* (EMI Records, 1994)! A mathematician utilising mathematics to power scientific thinking, while also developing celebrity status, is indeed a curious figure and one who himself stimulates curiosity in all of us.

Why is curiosity important in mathematics?

Problems in mathematics have intrigued people for centuries. Given the nature of the mathematical problems we encounter on a daily basis, most of us are able to (and expect to) solve mathematical puzzles within a short space of time, but it took over 350 years for anyone to provide a proof for Fermat's Last Theorem (often considered the most notorious problem in the history of mathematics!). But why do we bother? What is it that drives us to try to solve these mathematical conundrums? For a few people it will simply be to pass a test or to get a job, both of which are essential and useful goals. For most of us, solving a mathematical problem instils a sense of pride, from the accomplishment or the privilege of acquiring new knowledge. However, if we did not have curiosity to pursue some of these mathematical problems, we may, for example, not appreciate how the Golden Ratio is used to design aesthetically pleasing buildings or why it is likely that two children in the same class may share a birthday.

These motivations may partly explain our mathematical curiosity. But would most people select mathematics as a subject about which they are naturally curious? Is their mathematical curiosity limited to checking a price or change at the checkout? As teachers, should we promote greater and deeper curiosity about mathematics? Why is curiosity important to us? How will curiosity help people to pass a test, answer questions about their learning or develop a love of mathematics?

In Chapter 1 we shared Litman's (2005) definition of curiosity as 'a desire to know, to see, or to experience that motivates exploratory behaviour directed towards the acquisition of new information'. Like any subject, mathematics is about adding to our existing understanding and body of knowledge. However, we also outlined four different models of curiosity, which we can use to explore why capturing and exploiting curiosity in mathematics for learners is essential if we want mathematicians for the future, to enable either the next Einstein, Stephen Hawking or writer of *The Simpsons* (many of whom are themselves mathematicians).

The first model looked at the idea that curiosity is a specific human drive. Although perhaps the need to know and understand mathematics is not as powerful as the drive to eat or drink, when presented with mathematical scenarios children often find themselves drawn towards exploring the problem. For example, the need to know if two add two equals four each time is a curiosity in itself. Are there any situations where two added to two does not equal four? Could it be the uniformity and regularity of mathematics that makes it such a curious subject? Usually the mathematics that learners experience in primary school does always result in an answer, which perhaps gives us that drive and determination to always try to find it?

The second model explored in Chapter 1 wondered if curiosity is the result of violated expectations. If the first model of curiosity results from a drive to always find the answer, the second drive almost contradicts this in that some mathematics does not always produce the answer we are expecting. In this way curiosity is potentially evoked because our beliefs have been violated. In mathematics this can sometimes occur when misconceptions are uncovered and challenged. For example, if learners believe that when a number is multiplied by ten the original number changes only by a zero being added (e.g. $13 \times 10 = 130$), this view is then violated when we apply this rule to decimal numbers (e.g. $0.4 \times 10 \neq 0.40$). While often learners may not accept instantly that the rule does not work, their curiosity has been sparked by this discovery. A challenge can now be set to find other numbers that either obey or disobey the rule and are indeed in violation of our expectations.

The third model looked at whether curiosity can be considered a reference point. In other words, curiosity could be harnessed through the absence of information. In mathematics this could be trying to find the answer to what the eighth prime number is starting from zero, finding a missing number in a Fibonacci sequence, proving a conjecture that odd numbers added to odd numbers always total an even number or what the sides of an oblong could be with an area of 100 centimetres squared. This model of curiosity is interesting in that it suggests that in order to evoke curiosity we need to have some knowledge and interest in the subject matter. So, if learners are not particularly interested in finding Fibonacci numbers we may lose the moment to be curious. This could be an example of the need for a teacher to reveal potential patterns and stimulate questions for learners to cultivate curiosity behaviours.

The final model explored whether curiosity serves to seek and satisfy, and was suggested by Litman (2005) in an attempt to harness the other three models of curiosity. So perhaps the drive to find an answer to how many ... becomes a curiosity because of the need to know the answer, or that when engaging in the problem the answer is challenged due to new knowledge and existing understanding coming under attack. Either way, learners may not even recognise why they are curious. Does this matter? However, for teachers these different models are useful as they allow us to understand and potentially create opportunities to arouse mathematical curiosity.

The four models above draw on the notion that curiosity helps learners to acquire, refine, challenge and develop knowledge and understanding. In other words, the models use curiosity as a vehicle for intellectual response. Piaget (1958) also saw curiosity as a cognitive activity, which was derived from our intellectual need to make sense of the world. He suggested that curiosity is stimulated when there is a discrepancy between what you expect and what actually happens (which would fit with the model of curiosity violating expectation).

However, there are other reasons why curiosity is important in mathematics which link to an emotional response. Promoting curiosity in mathematics is a powerful concept particularly with the potential negative emotions attached to mathematics (Brown et al., 2008; Bibby, 2002; Nardi and Steward, 2003). If stimulating curiosity in mathematics leads to more children getting excited, this in turn helps to raise the profile of and engagement with mathematics and provides a hook to help engage children in the wonder and beauty of mathematics.

Teachers must see pupil curiosity as a significant ally in promoting pupil achievement too (for example, using ratios in genetics or the Fibonacci sequence in fractals). Much of the rationale given in this chapter to create opportunities for curiosity (for either an intellectual or emotional response) relies on learners being interested in the tasks set. We need to review which tasks learners get curious about and which they do not. Chapter 3 explores some activities and pedagogy that have the potential to spark this curiosity in children.

 Reflective activity

Take a moment to reflect on something that made you curious in mathematics. It could be as simple as a number, or a pattern, perhaps some shapes or a piece of data. What did that curiosity make you do? How did it shape your thinking? Did it make you want to forget about it or pursue it?

Some people may find the number 13 curious, because it provokes such a different reaction with people. It really does seem to be a love it or hate it number! This emotional attachment to a number makes me curious about its properties. As a teacher I can model mathematical curiosity and wonder about the frequency of 13 and its selection by players of the National Lottery, for example.

Skills in mathematics that are linked to/draw out curiosity

There are important skills that we use in mathematics which are synonymous with curiosity. For example, to:

- ask questions;
- search for patterns;

- find links;
- communicate;
- develop an enquiring mind;
- solve problems (as opposed to just being given answers).

It is often these pedagogic principles that are better for engaging curiosity in learners rather than a task which can be limiting and finite. As Engel (2015) points out, while babies and young children appear to be born with a desire to be curious, this quality 'rests in great part on the people and experiences that surround and shape a child's daily life'. As teachers, it is our duty to provide opportunities for learners to develop these skills to harness qualities that being curious about mathematics can potentially draw out. We might have a superb activity but opportunities to stimulate and build on skills to develop curiosity could be lost.

So, opportunities in mathematics lessons to promote skills in curiosity could involve:

- writing/solving a puzzle;
- seeking a solution to a problem;
- planning and carrying out an investigation;
- writing a conjecture;
- proving a conjecture;
- playing a mathematics game;
- employing a wide range of methods;
- using engaging contexts;
- exploring mathematics outside the classroom;
- challenging familiar ideas in mathematics;
- explaining mathematics to an alien;
- reasoning in mathematics;
- hot seating in mathematics;
- exploring layers of meaning in mathematics.

CASE STUDY

A mathematically curious classroom

I opened the door and peered inside – not into a classroom, but a castle with brick walls. In one corner was a banqueting table with chairs surrounding it and a wrought-iron chandelier suspended above it, while in the other corner swathes of material flapped from

Figure 2.2   Is it a classroom or a castle?

the ceiling. Children were sitting at the table, or lying on a carpet of gold or hiding in what appeared to be a dungeon, yet they all had one thing in common. They were all doubling numbers and recording their thinking and answers on their gold (not white) boards. They were all absorbed in their work and didn't even notice the curious face on the stranger entering the room. And I was curious, very curious. Was this mathematics? Where were the tables and chairs? Why was there a fake fire flickering on the interactive whiteboard instead of learning objectives and success criteria? This was a very different style of mathematics teaching and learning I had seen, and yet all the children were calculating numbers above their 'expected' level and were all on task and working independently. Is this one of the ways we capture curiosity in mathematics?

These children were clearly wrapped up in their mathematical work and when speaking to them they talked about their castle environment, where all their learning is immersed through this context. They showed impressive enthusiasm and they obviously loved their new look classroom! Chapter 10 focuses in even closer and reveals how this school has set up their whole curriculum so that it is one which promotes creative and curious children who love to learn and succeed.

Reflective activity

While we don't all have to turn our classrooms into castles to find curiosity in mathematics, consider what makes your classroom a curious place for mathematical learning.

A curious classroom might also take the mathematical learning outside. Using the outdoors is a great way to inspire and interest children, both traits of curiosity. However, a curious classroom could also be created through different pedagogical styles as opposed to a physical change in the classroom.

So perhaps setting up a mathematically curious classroom is partly about the tasks that we give children. Clearly, there are different types of tasks and activities that we use in the classroom. Schmidt et al. (2002) identified the intended curriculum, the implemented curriculum and the attained curriculum. There are certainly moments in mathematics where children have to be taught certain knowledge and skills to ensure they achieve understanding and age-related objectives and pass statutory tests. However, perhaps tasks that are too often directive or teaching that is too instrumental (Skemp, 1976) results in answers being given without much thought and without the chance to be curious.

So, how should we plan and organise our classrooms to spark mathematical curiosity? Duckworth (1972) warns against the classroom which is too tidy and too ordered, but this doesn't mean we have to throw out the order either. Perhaps we can plan and organise mathematics lessons and experiences to promote mathematical curiosity by:

- ensuring all are happy to take a risk;
- the teacher modelling mathematical risk taking;
- mathematical displays and interactive artefacts;
- mathematics in our topics and in other subjects;
- promoting a curiosity wizard (Can I explain? Can I reason with this mathematics? Does it apply in all situations? Can I apply it in two or three other subjects? Can I prove the mathematics wrong?).

However, perhaps one of the most powerful ways to teach the skills of curiosity in mathematics is to be curious yourself.

Conclusion

As with the other Primary STEM subjects in this book, mathematics is also a platform from which curiosity can spring. This chapter has shown how mathematics can be found in each of the four models of curiosity explored in Chapter 1 if we know how to recognise and exploit it. It has explored some of the skills we use in mathematics and suggested a variety of ways to evoke curiosity in mathematics.

Chapter summary

Having read this chapter you will:

- know how mathematics fits into the four models of curiosity identified in Chapter 1;
- know why it is important to cultivate curiosity within mathematics;
- be clear about the skills used in mathematics to promote curiosity;
- be curious about the second mathematics chapter in this book!

CHAPTER 3

WAYS TO ENHANCE CURIOSITY IN PRIMARY MATHEMATICS

Chapter objectives

After reading this chapter you will:

- have a toolkit of ideas with which to promote mathematical curiosity in the classroom;
- know what pedagogical techniques inspire learners to be mathematically curious;
- be curious yourself about trying out some of the mathematical activities.

Overview

Young learners begin school as curious and interested mathematicians. They are full of questions such as what is the biggest number? How many stars are there in the sky? Why is the number five odd and the number six even? According to Mason et al. (2005) learners are born with mathematical powers that support and aid them in their mathematical quests (powers such as organising and classifying or imagining and expressing). We will explore these mathematical powers later on in this chapter but we need to harness and use and extend these early beginnings of curiosity that learners have before it is diluted, damaged or erased. Using mathematical powers may be one way to continue the curiosity in mathematics but there are other things we can do too.

We are lucky. Humans have mathematics. Mathematics is all around us. As humans we all have a ready-made culture in which creating mathematical thinking and sparking mathematical curiosity is on tap. Much of the play learners engage in before they start school is rich in mathematics, whether it is playing shopkeeper or building towers of bricks. Most learners start school mathematically equipped having engaged in mathematical experiences, whether they were aware of these or not. Our job as teachers is to continue to create exciting and curious mathematical opportunities to engage and inspire the young mathematicians of the future.

 Reflective activity

Take a moment to consider this question: if humans had not discovered mathematics, would mathematics exist?

Of course, mathematics would exist in nature (e.g. Fibonacci numbers) but without it we would be unable to appreciate the beauty of mathematical relationships or explore the power of mathematics in its numerous applications (e.g. buildings, science, nutrition, arts, etc.). Everywhere we look mathematics exists. It is about ideas, connections and relationships that help us make sense of the world. At the heart of mathematics is pattern. If we look at the world through mathematical glasses we will see pattern everywhere. Pattern has helped people to navigate oceans, to plan space missions, to build social media and create scientific knowledge. Devlin (1997) writes that 'there is scarcely any aspect of our lives that is not affected, to a greater or lesser extent, by mathematics; for abstract patterns are the very essence of thought, of communication, of computation, of society, and of life itself'.

So, what kinds of mathematical activities and problems can we use in the classroom to spark curiosity in mathematics? What tasks create that insatiable curiosity and that ability to learn from each other? At what point in a task do you get curious? Chapter 2 explored why curiosity is important in mathematics. This chapter offers a plethora of activities and tasks, alongside pedagogical strategies, that help to spark this curiosity in mathematics.

Promoting curiosity in primary mathematics

One of the easiest ways to promote curiosity in mathematics is to model mathematical curiosity yourself. Teachers are all role models to their learners and so it is up to us to present mathematics as curious, interesting and enjoyable. Negative attitudes (such as boredom, frustration or a lack of enthusiasm) are hardly going to inspire learners to want to engage in mathematical activities and are probably not going to cultivate a curiosity for it. Chapter 1 explored the different models which seek to explain human curiosity (while Chapter 2 perceived these motivations through mathematical lenses), but this is not the most important factor. Being curious is.

 Reflective activity

Take a moment to consider what would discourage you from being mathematically curious. What type of activity or pedagogy would begin to limit your enthusiasm and willingness to engage in a task?

The above question will stimulate a range of responses. For some it will be working individually, or perhaps wading through repetitive questions in a textbook or on a worksheet. Perhaps the thought of never finding the answer or needing to find more than one answer affects our mathematical resolve.

However, the eight points below list some of the quick ways we can try to arrest any potential disaffection with mathematics and build up a mathematical toolkit of skills to help learners be curious about mathematics, and thus have the determination, resolve and enthusiasm to love it.

1. Low-threshold, high-ceiling tasks

Give learners rich mathematical tasks, often called 'low threshold, high ceiling tasks' (McClure, 2011). These are tasks that all learners can access and work on at their own level but the task itself has many different possibilities for learners to pursue. One of the advantages in all learners working on the same task (apart from not being lonely) is that everyone feels equal but at the same time high achievers can challenge themselves while the less confident can work at their level and pace. As a result of learners sharing their approaches and strategies to the task and solution a sense of community is established and often learners hear strategies they may not have heard if the class were organised in a different way or different tasks were given out to groups of learners. Finally, these types of tasks usually focus on the mathematical skills required to solve the problem, rather than the content needed. The level of thinking these tasks draw out is often sophisticated and eloquent, and certainly above the content knowledge required. Thus, these tasks help to show learners that mathematics is more about the way we approach and think about a problem, rather than just the content knowledge needed to solve it. The nrich website (www.nrich.maths.org) has thousands of 'low-threshold, high-ceiling tasks' but my favourites are still problems such as *Strike it out, Noah* and *I'm Eight*.

2. Fluency, reasoning and problem solving

The three aims of the new mathematics National Curriculum (DfE, 2013) encourage as much of our mathematics teaching and learning to be filtered through fluency, reasoning and problem solving. As teachers, we seek activities which draw on each of these aims within a curious and interesting context.

Ask learners (of any age) to draw a blank number line. In pairs, one partner decides on the beginning and end of the line (e.g. 0 and 10, 1 and 20, 37 and 64, 0.3 and 7) and then asks their partner to place numbers on the line (usually four or five numbers is sufficient). The pupil placing the numbers has to draw on their fluency skills of where the numbers fit, in relation to the proportion of the line, reason and justify why they have placed the number in that position and draw on problem-solving skills (such as working out key facts to help them, e.g. what would half of the line be?) to complete the task.

When I have tried this activity with both learners and adults I have observed great delight from the person setting up the activity (which is always harder than the teacher would set!), and amazing resilience and perseverance from the person trying to work out where the numbers fit. The curiosity arises from the numbers selected and their placement on the line.

3. This is the answer, what is the question?

Give learners the answer so they have to find the question (e.g. the answer is 10, what could the question be?). This activity helps to remove the perception that the answer in mathematics is always the goal. It also shows learners that there can often be more than one answer (or more than one way of reaching the answer) to a problem. For those learners who worry about being right in mathematics this activity shows that everyone can be right and helps to potentially spark a curiosity in trying to find the most unusual question, the hardest question or the funniest question to finding the answer. Here are some answers that you could ask your learners to find the (possible) questions to:

The answer is ½, what is the question?

The answer is a tetrahedron, what is the question?

The answer is an odd number, what is the question?

The answer is less than 100, but it is not a prime or square number, what is the question?

4. Let's talk!

Promote the use of talk in mathematics lessons. Mathematics is a language that enables us to describe and explain situations, to think logically and offer conjectures to communicate ideas with precision. Learners need to learn the language of mathematics. Expecting learners to talk, and explain their work, helps them to understand it better and be more confident about it. Using mathematical vocabulary is an important part of any mathematics lesson, but learners love using words that sound strange or unusual. Using these types of words not only helps to strengthen mathematical knowledge but could help to maintain a level of curiosity about the subject too. Here are a few words to get you started:

Isosceles • Cardinality • Hypotenuse • Factorial • Infinite •

Vulgar • Truncate • Trapezium • Array

5. Group problem-solving tasks

This is a pedagogical approach that supports learners' development of problem-solving skills, but also strengthens their listening skills, knowing when to ask questions, taking turns and allocation of roles (e.g. who will record, who will feedback?). The group has one task between them to solve. This activity can be planned in several ways. One way is to give the group the problem and then allow them to decide how to solve it. *Dice in a Corner* (www.nrich.maths.org) is a good problem to try in a group. Give the group a pile of 1–6 dice and ask them to stack two, three or four dice on top of each other. The only rule is that where two faces from different dice touch, they must be the same numbers. Another approach is to write the problem on several pieces of paper that are given out to each member of the group, who then has to read them out, while the group decide if the information contained on each piece is relevant or not. Here is a tried-and-tested one:

Your mission is to build a column of six cubes.

There are six different colours in the column.

The red cube is between the pink and blue cube.

The black cube is between the blue cube and the red cube.

The green cube is between the blue cube and the yellow cube.

The blue cube is between the black cube and the yellow cube.

The yellow and pink cubes are not between any cubes.

The red cube is next to the top cube.

Was your mission successful?

6. Design your task

This pedagogical approach encourages learners to create their own tasks for each other to solve and in doing so become active in their learning. Sometimes learners are only receivers of information, and have little opportunity for more direct participation. This may not be a conducive strategy to instil curiosity for many. For some learners, mathematics could be a discipline that is done to them, rather than being a creative and curious subject to explore. Writing mathematical tasks offers learners an opportunity to take part in the lesson and own the task.

There are several different starting points to support learners in designing their own tasks. You could ask them to choose some mathematical equipment (e.g. Numicon©, cubes, counters) and then ask them to write a problem using this. For example, create a repeating pattern using cubes or how many different ways can you make 100 using different Numicon© tiles? Another starting point is to chose a number (e.g. 7, 43, 0.6) and then pose a problem which either uses this number in the question or uses this number as the answer. These two tasks could be quite short, so why not challenge the learners to write a longer task, such as to find out the percentage of the world's population living in each country or continent.

When learners are designers of their own tasks they become the most powerful teacher. We are helping them to become mini mathematicians in their own right.

7. Longer investigations

Sometimes the mathematics we do in the classroom consists of short tasks that learners finish by the end of the lesson. While these serve a purpose, they may not help to embrace a curiosity that is longitudinal or lasting. It is the hunger for knowledge that can often make us curious and willing to persevere. Engel (2015) points out that 'in order to flourish, curiosity needs to be cultivated'. For some learners a task that they need to return to and persevere at engenders this curiosity.

So, why not consider setting learners a mathematical problem that lasts over several days or even weeks? You may only give them a few minutes each day to think about the problem, but this is helpful in showing them that we do not always complete tasks or questions within the time frame of the lesson. Longer tasks could include:

- How many different ways can you make 99 using any operation?
- There are only five ways to construct a three-dimensional solid using regular polygons. Is this true?
- How many shapes can you make using five squares?
- Who is taller: you or an Emperor Penguin?

8. Asking curious questions

There are questions (e.g. what is the product of three and four?) and then there are curious questions (e.g. how do you know parallel lines continue infinitely?). We need a balance of both types of questions but the latter are often the ones which help to stimulate curious learners. Here are a few questions to set alight that curiosity:

Do all shapes tessellate?

What is the biggest number you know?

If you cut a piece off a 2D shape does its perimeter reduce?

Is there any way I can win the Lottery?

We can also challenge learners by not asking questions, but giving them mathematical statements to prove or disprove. Learners can decide whether the statements are always true, sometimes true or never true. Explanations usually involve generating examples and counterexamples. This activity helps to develop learners' capacity to explain, convince and prove, while drawing them into a world of mathematical curiosity. Here are some statements to try out.

Multiplying makes numbers bigger.

Numbers with more digits are greater in value.

Zero always means nothing.

Shapes with large areas have large perimeters.

Promoting curiosity in mathematics is …?

This section considers pedagogical approaches that can help to cultivate and maintain levels of curiosity in mathematics.

Curiosity in mathematics is … knowing when to leave learners alone

As teachers we want to teach. We feel it is our role and our duty. But sometimes some of the best teaching is that which takes place behind the scenes – in other words, on the planning page. Take the example of the Year 1 and 2 lesson below.

CASE STUDY

Cuisenaire rods

The learners quickly settled on the carpet as they always did at the start of the mathematics lesson. However, no learning objective was written on the board or verbally shared with them. Instead, small red boxes were handed out and the learners were instructed to investigate in pairs. Inside the box were different lengths of coloured rods. After a few minutes of exploring the teacher held up an orange rod and challenged the learners to make as many different 'trains' with the other rods that would equal the length of the orange rod. It was a simple instruction and yet the buzz and noise in the room would give the impression to outsiders that very important problems were being solved. The lesson lasted over an hour and only occasionally were the learners halted in their investigations to be reminded to record their thinking (in what ever form they desired). A brief plenary revealed a wealth of trains or rods had been discovered (not all equal in length, but this served as another opportunity to extend thinking). Learners had been asked to use the word 'conjecture' during the task and were thrilled in reporting back 'My conjecture that you can make 5 trains is correct' or 'I conjecture I can make 10 rods'.

In the above lesson learners were excited, curious and explored mathematical thinking for over an hour. Yet the lesson was set up in

(Continued)

(Continued)

Figure 3.1 An example of different 'Cuisenaire' trains

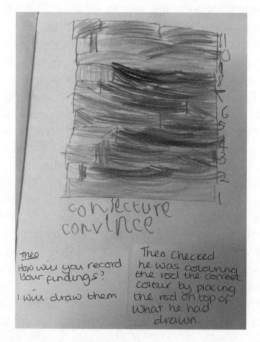

Figure 3.2 An example of one learner's thinking

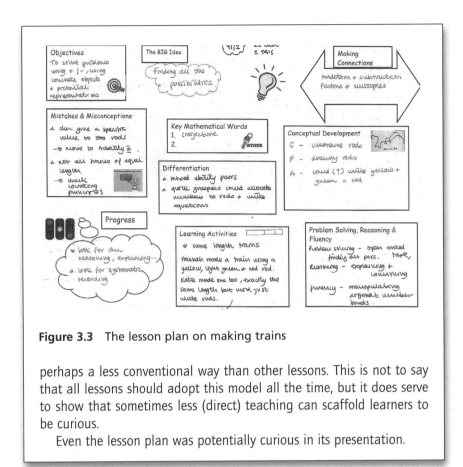

Figure 3.3 The lesson plan on making trains

perhaps a less conventional way than other lessons. This is not to say that all lessons should adopt this model all the time, but it does serve to show that sometimes less (direct) teaching can scaffold learners to be curious.

Even the lesson plan was potentially curious in its presentation.

Curiosity in mathematics ... is creating the deliberately difficult path

It may seem a contradiction to suggest that challenging learners and deliberately creating obstacles could cultivate curiosity, yet confidence, persistence and learning are not mastered through giving learners low-level, easy work that they can do without much thought. Work that is too easy is often not challenging and lacks the motivation and interest to maintain the curiosity to finish it or pursue it further.

Piaget (1958) was among those who rejected the idea of memorising procedures, believing that true learning is about making sense of ideas and where they fit within our existing frames of knowledge. He suggested that when our ideas fit together and make sense, we are in a state of equilibrium. However, when we encounter new ideas that do not fit into our current models we enter a state Piaget called disequilibrium. While this sounds uncomfortable, Piaget believed that a person in disequilibrium finds true wisdom and it is essential to learning.

This disequilibrium could tap into learners' curiosity too. Ask learners to represent the following two calculations using multilink cubes: 3×4 and $12 \div 4$. They will probably already know the answer and may even be frustrated at having to represent it this way. However, the ability to represent and reason abstract parts of mathematics (like calculations) develops our understanding and hopefully curiosity of it. Using the multilink cubes deliberately chooses the difficult path but ultimately results in greater understanding.

Curiosity in mathematics ... is making mistakes

As mentioned in Chapter 1, research has shown that when we make mistakes our brains 'spark and grow' (Boaler, 2016). Scientific studies (Moser et al., 2011) have shown that when we make a mistake our brain has two potential responses. The first response (called an ERN response) happens when the brain experiences cognitive conflict between a correct answer and an error. Remarkably, this response happens even if the person is not aware of the mistake. The second response (called a Pe response) occurs when there is conscious reflection on the mistake.

The importance of making mistakes is part of the research on fixed and growth mindset (Dweck, 2006), which was mentioned in Chapter 1. This is the notion that all of us with a growth (rather than a fixed) mindset can succeed at mathematics, if we are prepared to work hard, view mistakes as a challenge and have the motivation to learn. However, learners with a fixed mindset believe they are either good at mathematics or not. Powerful research showed that having a fixed mindset is one of the reasons that girls in particular opt out of STEM subjects (Boaler, 2014). Even if girls believe they are good at mathematics, research shows they are afraid of continuing in case they make a mistake and are no longer seen to be clever. The tests that the Program for International Student Assessment (PISA) team administer every four years showed that in 2012 learners with a growth mindset outperformed those with a fixed mindset in mathematics (PISA, 2012).

Yet making mistakes in mathematics is an area that teachers and learners have previously tried to avoid, so we need to show learners that mistakes are valuable. This may be tough! Trying to convince learners that the more mistakes they make the better they could be at mathematics seems at odds with trying to find the right answer and working efficiently. Below are two case studies where mistakes or different lines of thinking have enabled and helped to maintain high levels of curiosity about the mathematics.

CASE STUDY

Show me

Mini whiteboards are common in classrooms, with all learners writing a response to a question on them and then sharing their thinking with the rest of the class. In this lesson the teacher asked the learners to show a quadrilateral with two lines of symmetry. The teacher then recorded several different responses on the board, both those that were correct and incorrect. She then challenged learners to explore which were the correct responses.

Using this pedagogical technique values all answers from learners. It also removes the need to always find the right answer. When talking to the learners, one of them said that he likes to offer an incorrect response, because 'it makes the lesson more interesting'.

CASE STUDY

Odd one out

In this activity learners are given three objects or numbers to consider. Their task is to decide which is the odd one out. In some cases the teacher has decided prior to the task, but you can decide whether to stick to your original choice or change your mind! In the example below, learners are given the numbers 8, 5 and 24. They then decide which number is the odd one out, and why. Do you agree with them?

(Continued)

(Continued)

Figure 3.4 Odd one out activity

Curiosity in mathematics … is creating the right conditions for learning

 Reflective activity

Look at figures 3.5 and 3.6. Which classroom appeals to you the most? Which do you want to jump into and take part in the learning?

Of course, not all twenty-first-century classrooms look like figure 3.6, yet the photograph serves to make us consider the type of environment that helps to spark curiosity. As well as the mathematical equipment and iPads learners now use in modern schools, the second classroom shows learners working away from their desks and in relaxed groups, as opposed to sitting formally in rows.

Often one of the easiest ways to start a lesson and engage learners' curiosity is to break with conformity and start in a different way. This may be a different location, for example, in the hall or outside.

Figure 3.5   A Victorian classroom

Figure 3.6   An example of a twenty-first-century classroom

It is also important, despite some of our adult reluctance at times, to try to keep up to date with what learners are interested in. If Star Wars© or Minecraft© are the latest crazes, this can be a reliable way of engaging learners' curiosity in their learning. So, for those who are now curious about how Star Wars© can link with mathematics, here is an activity to try out.

STEM link
to computing

Reflective activity

Star Wars© mathematics

The Death Star *was the Empire's ultimate weapon, a space station the size of a small moon! There are various facts and figures about the size, shape, cost of the fictional* Death Star *and this activity does not require the facts to be correct. So, according to one website (www.en.m.wikipedia.org) the following data is provided:*

- *it had a crew of 265,675;*
- *52,276 gunners;*
- *607,360 troops;*
- *30,984 stormtroopers;*
- *42,782 ship support staff;*
- *180,216 pilots;*
- *a diameter of between 140 and 160km.*

Perhaps for some learners just adding up the Star Wars© numbers is more exciting and curious than adding numbers in abstract or that have no interest to them. They could work out how many personnel were thought to be on board the Death Star. *However, they could also work out how many levels or floors it could have, using the diameter as a guide and then try to work out how many personnel could fit on to each floor comfortably. Ask learners which of our planets is the closest in size to the* Death Star, *and perhaps when making models of the planets, they could make another model to include the* Death Star.

Figure 3.7 One learner's drawing of the *Death Star*

Curiosity in mathematics ... is using mathematical powers

At the beginning of this chapter we considered the possibility that all learners are born with natural mathematical powers (Mason et al., 2005), which they can all use and exploit in mathematics lessons. Learners demonstrate from a very early age that they have the ability to make and test conjectures, to generalise and to make sense of their experiences. They are able to imagine, and express their ideas, to collect and classify information and to convince someone of their results. According to Mason et al. (2005), there are four sets of mathematical powers:

- imagining and expressing;
- specialising and generalising;
- conjecturing and convincing; and
- organising and classifying.

All learners can imagine and then express their ideas, either through words, pictures, actions, numbers, etc. The power of imagination is the power to think about what is not actually there. When we look at a pattern we can imagine how it may start or continue. We can then express this by drawing the pattern or writing it down. Being able to imagine draws on our desire to be curious, to want to discover more, while being able to express allows us to communicate with others.

From a very young age learners use generalisations to make sense of their world, using specialist examples to identify specific objects. For example, learners very quickly understand which animal is a dog. They generalise that all four-legged creatures with a tail and a bark are dogs. It is only when they need to distinguish between one breed and another that they begin to offer specialist examples. In mathematics it would be impossible to learn every odd number that exists, so instead we choose some specialist examples that fit with our generalised understanding of what constitutes any odd number. This mathematical power encourages learners to offer and test conjectures, which they can first generalise, and then find specialist examples to make sense of the general. The desire to find a particular case that fits both a general and more specific case can be a catalyst for being curious.

To offer a conjecture about something is to think out loud and then test out and convince others of your theory. Learners need to be busy in developing their own ideas. These sparks of ideas are sparks of curiosity that we can then encourage them to take further. The power of offering a conjecture is that a conjecture is never wrong; it may just need to be modified. This removes the pressure of trying to find answers that are either right or wrong. If we value conjectures thinking will flourish.

We all have the desire to organise and classify, and learners come to school with this power already, whether it is through organising and classifying the train set, the miniature tea party or putting away the dishes after tea. Organising reduces confusion and in a curious world we can sometimes become lost in our direction of thought. This power helps us to sort and classify our thinking, which in turn allows us to refine our thinking and extend it.

The mathematical powers provide learners, with a different way of experiencing mathematics. If we want learners to be curious about mathematics we need to give them different ways of thinking about it. As Piggott and Back (2011) said, 'a problem is only a problem when you cannot do it'. When some schools have introduced the mathematical powers to learners, the children have designed super hero characters to represent each pair of powers, as the photograph from one classroom in Figure 3.8 shows.

Figure 3.8 Mathematical powers designed by learners in one school

STEM link to design and technology

Curiosity in mathematics ... is connections within mathematics and with other subjects

In mathematics, making connections to other areas of mathematics is vital to see how mathematics itself is interlinked. Learners often find it difficult to generalise and transfer learning to other areas in mathematics. Related topics such as division and fractions can remain unconnected. Connecting mathematics in this way helps to build bridges between mathematical ideas and also serves for learners to see how they can use their existing

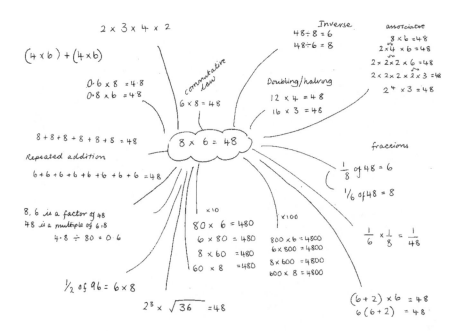

Figure 3.9 If you know that 8 × 6 = 48, what else do you know?

knowledge to create new knowledge. Ask learners to write the equation 8 × 6 = 48 in the middle of a piece of paper. Now ask them what else do you know (and why)? With this task learners may use arithmetical laws of commutativity, inverse, equivalence, etc. in order to 'map' their knowledge.

This 'connectionist' (Askew et al., 1997) view of teaching and learning emphasises the interconnected nature of the subject. Many researchers (e.g. Swan, 2005) see the teacher as having a more proactive role using this style of teaching, in comparison to that of 'discovery' teaching, where the teacher simply presents tasks and expects learners to explore and discover ideas for themselves. However, both models have merits in cultivating curious learners.

However, it is also useful to see how mathematics connects to other subjects, which helps learners to see mathematics in the world around them. This may draw on other primary school subjects such as English. One medium used in English is the quantity of fiction books learners have access to. There are many texts which use mathematics, either in an obvious way (e.g. perhaps a number is part of the title of the book) or in discrete ways (e.g. ordering and classifying letters to post). For those learners who are a little more reluctant to engage and become curious about mathematics, using a fiction book may be a different approach to see the beauty, relevance and applicability of the subject.

Figure 3.10 Using fiction books as curious starting points

Science is another subject that gives primary learners plenty of opportunities to see the connections and links to mathematics. For many people, the link between mathematics and science is intuitive and obvious (Cross and Borthwick, 2016). How can we do any science without doing any mathematics? Yet we need to make these links explicit to learners.

The primary STEM subjects all need and use mathematics. We could be studying how different animals use mathematics in science (e.g. a spider spinning a spiral web or dolphins communicating through sound waves), how to make a waterproof, robust and safe shelter for your magical creature in design and technology or how to program the Bee Bot© across the assault course in as few a moves as possible. There will be learners who just love mathematics for what it is. However, there will also be those who are hesitant about mathematics, perhaps holding misconceptions about the subject – that is hard, boring, difficult and not relevant. Connecting mathematics to other subject areas can dispel these myths. Find a context that inspires and excites learners. Once you have piqued their curiosity show them the mathematics hidden beneath!

Curiosity in mathematics is … finding an area that learners
find curious

At the beginning of this chapter we reflected upon what would
stop us being curious in mathematics. This section now considers what area within mathematics might make us curious, and
more importantly what learners may find curious. It will be
different for everyone, but here are some ideas to try out with
your learners.

- Find out which numbers are happy and which are sad.
- Which shapes tessellate and which do not?
- Which is the biggest number you know (e.g. is it a Googolplex?).
  Can you write it? Draw a picture to represent it?
- Is it possible to win the National Lottery?
- Are all squares rectangles?
- When do the hands of a clock coincide?
- Choose a number, shape or symbol that you are curious about.
  Find out as much as possible about it.

Figure 3.11 One class chose the number 0.5 as their curious number about
which they would discover more

Conclusion

This chapter offers some mathematical activities and pedagogical strategies that are tried and tested to appeal to learners to help to maintain the mathematical curiosity they have when they start school. Studies have shown that the teacher has the greatest impact on children's learning (Darling-Hammond, 2000), with the curriculum being another critical part of this responsibility. So, as teachers we are the ones who can give learners exciting mathematics that stimulates their curiosity and interest in mathematics. Jo Boaler (2016) talks about the 5Cs in mathematics – connection making, challenge, creativity, collaboration, and of course, curiosity. We can inspire learners to become curious about mathematics by being curious ourselves and providing an exciting mathematics curriculum that shows the importance of mathematics in the world.

Chapter summary

Having read this chapter you will:

- have a wide and varied resource pool to draw on to stimulate curiosity in mathematics;
- know how to develop mini mathematicians who are curious and creative;
- be inspired to design, create and adapt tasks which are catalysts for curiosity in mathematics and beyond.

CHAPTER 4

CURIOUS LEARNERS IN PRIMARY SCIENCE

CURIOSITY IS THE ENGINE OF ACHIEVEMENT

KEN ROBINSON

Chapter objectives

After reading this chapter you will:

*   appreciate how curiosity can be instrumental in scientific discovery and investigation;
*   have an understanding of how curiosity drives the scientific process;
*   be aware of strategies to develop learners' curiosity in science.

Overview

One of the key purposes of studying science at school, as stated in the English National Curriculum (DfE, 2013), is to develop a sense of excitement and curiosity about natural phenomena. Ofsted's 2013 report on science in schools entitled *Maintaining Curiosity* (Ofsted, 2013) asserts that the most successful teachers of primary science maintain pupils' curiosity and that the most successful schools have adopted this as one of their key principles.

Chapters 1 and 2 referred to the importance of a growth mindset (Dweck, 2006). Science and curiosity about the world encourage a personal growth mindset as learners experience the pleasure of learning.

Human curiosity is the key driver of the STEM subjects including science. Our curiosity leads us to ask questions about the world so we then have the possibility to make scientific discoveries. Many problems of the past, such as long-distance communication and safe lighting and heating for our homes, have been solved by curious scientists and engineers. Society needs children who grow up curious about the world. They are the ones likely to find solutions to the problems of global warming, energy use and feeding an ever-growing population. These are unavoidable challenges for the future; solutions and their realisation will come from the STEM subjects.

A scientist

Mary Anning was born to a poor family in Lyme Regis in 1799. She was one of ten children but only her older brother Joseph, along with Mary herself, survived childhood. She was lucky to escape common life-threatening diseases of the time such as smallpox and measles. Aged fifteen months, she even survived a lightning strike. While the lightning killed all three women looking after her, Mary appeared to benefit from the shock; though she was often pale and sick beforehand, it was said that the lightning seemed to furnish her with better health and vigour for life. Mary would collect the intriguingly shaped rocks she found on the beach below the cliffs to sell to rich Victorians. These 'curios' were not recognised as fossils at the time and were given informal names; 'verteberries' were fossilised vertebrae and 'snake-stones' were ammonites. Mary, however, was curious; how could snakes turn into stone? There were no snakes living in that part of the world anyway.

Mary's curiosity led her to become much more than a fossil collector. She taught herself about palaeontology from scientific papers often borrowed and copied out by hand. But she also learnt by investigation, dissecting sea creatures to improve her understanding of anatomy and bone structure in particular. Mary Anning's self-education and experience was such that important geologists such as William Buckland and Richard Owen would visit her to hunt fossils and discuss anatomy and classification. Even Richard Lyell and Charles Darwin became correspondents.

Figure 4.1   A Snake-stone or ammonite

In 2015, this token, given to Mary Anning on her 11th birthday, was found on Lyme Regis beach by a treasure hunter with a metal detector. Curiosity sometimes leads us to discover the unexpected. Find out more about Mary Anning at: www.bbc.in/1ofexU5

Figure 4.2   Mary Anning's birthday token

Photo © Michael Applegate/Lyme Regis Museum

Mary Anning's curiosity is perhaps best explained by Loewenstein's reference point model (Loewenstein, 1994), which can be thought of as a jigsaw. When we can see there is a picture, or an idea that is incomplete in our minds and we find some pieces that we think will match, we are keen to try to fit them to our previous understanding to create a more complete picture. For Mary Anning, the fossils that surrounded her every day were the missing pieces that held hidden answers to the questions in her mind. She taught herself to read the fossils and every new discovery provided a deeper and clearer understanding. Curiosity was Mary Anning's main tool. She had very little basic education and certainly no training in science. Yet her curiosity led her to question the explanations given for the 'curios' and she ending up making a major contribution to our understanding of evolution.

 Reflective activity

In which areas of science do you find yourself the most curious? Is it, like Mary Anning, the aspects you deal with every day such as how the brain works or how different foods might affect your body, or is it the far more distant and inaccessible topics such as black holes or quantum physics?

Why is curiosity important in science?

Edward Jenner is well known as the inventor of vaccination, a process that has saved millions from the fatal disease smallpox. His discovery was born of curiosity but it is interesting to note where that curiosity came from. It was not entirely his own. As early as 1763 John Fewster had given a talk to the London Medical Society reporting that a similar, but much weaker, disease called cowpox appeared to give protection from smallpox but he seems to have never tested the theory with his own investigation (Hopkins, 2002). John Fewster was a friend of Jenner and at meetings of the Convivio-Medical Society at *The Ship Inn* in Alveston, Gloucestershire, he repeatedly urged his colleagues to research his theory (Creighton, 1889). However, no investigation was forthcoming. Even in his personal interest in zoology Jenner's curiosity appeared limited. He exchanged many letters with his former teacher and great friend, the London surgeon John Hunter, founder of the Hunterian Museum. Hunter was pivotal in encouraging Jenner to develop his curiosity into practical experiments. In 1775 he replied to Jenner regarding a question about hedgehogs, encouraging him to do a practical experiment to establish the answer.

> *I thank you for your Expt on the Hedge Hog, but why do you ask me a question, by the way of solving it. I think your solution is just; but why think, why not trie the Expt.* (Extract from Hunter's reply to Jenner, 1775. www.jennermuseum.com, 2015)

It was not until 14 May 1796 that Jenner's curiosity led him to famously test John Fewster's theory. He used a knife to remove some of the puss from the cowpox blisters on the hand of a milkmaid called Sarah Nelmes. He used the puss to infect the 8-year-old son of his gardener, a boy named James Phipps, with cowpox. James developed a slight fever but nothing more. Later Jenner inoculated James with smallpox matter but James appeared immune. He did not even seem to be affected by a later attempt at a second inoculation. Jenner went on to test the process on 23 other people. Interestingly, at the time, medical trials were rare and many doctors would simply use their own experience and intuition to develop treatments. Maybe then it is less surprising that it took so long for Jenner's curiosity to get him as far as the experiment. Many would argue that his greatest achievement was not the initial discovery but in his diligent proof that the process led to immunity (Hopkins, 2002). Jenner was curious but it was his mentors, John Hunter and John Fewster, who encouraged him to develop his curiosity to a stage where he could establish an experimental proof.

Clearly, curiosity is essential in many aspects of science not simply in asking the questions in the first place. Mary Anning was curious to the point of obsession. It was a passion that drove her career. Luckily, her curiosity was matched by her determination to learn. Edward Jenner, however, was far more circumspect. He used his curiosity selectively to target problems that he could see would be of great value to solve. His example also demonstrates that curiosity can be fostered and encouraged in others. But where does curiosity fit with learning science in the primary classroom? And what is the value of controlling curiosity as Jenner did? Would we not learn more if we let our curiosity run free?

To exploit the links with primary science teaching we need to consider the process of scientific enquiry. How does science work?

Skills in science that are linked to/draw out curiosity

It is said that science is the process of asking and finding answers to questions. There are different ways to find answers and these are noted as methods of enquiry in the National Curriculum: fair testing; observing changes over time; identification and classification; pattern spotting and research using secondary sources (DfE, 2013). The method chosen will be determined by the question itself. For example, the question 'which of these paper towels is the most absorbent?' is best solved by carrying out a fair test but 'which of the planets is the largest?' can only be answered in the classroom by research using secondary sources. Some questions such as 'do plants need light to grow?' could easily be researched, but more valuable, first-hand experience can be obtained by setting up an experiment and observing changes over time.

Curiosity is usually the initial driver in asking the scientific question in the first place but it is also present throughout the science process cycle (Figure 4.3). Curiosity is clearly involved in deciding which enquiry method to use and also in

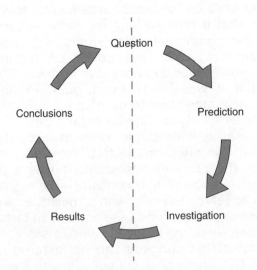

Figure 4.3 The science process cycle

planning the investigation and choosing equipment, but logic and reasoning are very significant at this stage. Curiosity is equally evident after measurements or observations have been taken and the process of making a conclusion begins. This is curiosity about the scientific process itself. Here there are many questions to be asked: Are these measurements reliable? Is there a pattern in the way the numbers change? Is that what was predicted? Curiosity about the results and conclusions will often lead to further questions, 'why does a plant need light to grow?' for example, and these clearly lead to further enquiry to find deeper answers.

STEM link to mathematics

The process of science can be considered as a cycle (see Figure 4.3). Curiosity occurs at every stage in the cycle but it might be true to say that, on the right-hand side, curiosity about the world drives the process. Perhaps, as learners move to the left-hand side, curiosity about the results drives a move towards an answer and perhaps a new question? Research scientists may go around this cycle several times as they focus in on a problem and seek an answer. Typically, in a classroom, primary learners investigate a question but rarely have the opportunity to determine a new question and pursue that question further. However, this is required in the National Curriculum (DfE, 2013), the programme of study states that learners in Years 5 and 6 should be taught the working scientifically skill of 'using test results to make predictions to set up further comparative and fair tests'. One effective method of making this happen lies in reviewing graphical data. The pictorial representation of data presented by a graph or chart is often easier to interpret and analyse than numerical data and, as a consequence, more accessible to learners. Data loggers allow even younger learners to create accurate line graphs, which can then be reviewed and questioned. The example below was created by measuring the temperature both inside and outside a Year 4 classroom for 48 hours (see Figure 4.4).

STEM link to mathematics

The learners were curious about the graph, wanting to know why there were various little dips in the line and why the indoor temperature decreased smoothly before suddenly increasing. This second question led to a discussion about central heating and how it came on each morning to warm the classroom. The learners were then curious to know how hot the radiators would get, so a second investigation was set up to compare the radiator temperature with the room temperature (Figure 4.5). Again, on seeing the graph, the learners asked questions about why the radiators got hotter more quickly than the room and why the room did not get as hot as the radiators.

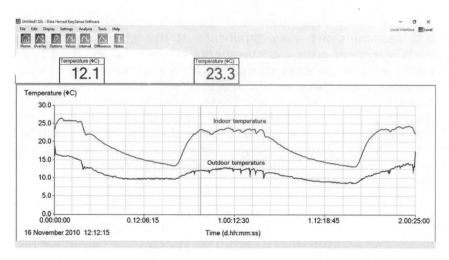

Figure 4.4   A graph of indoor and outdoor temperatures over two days

STEM link
to
mathematics

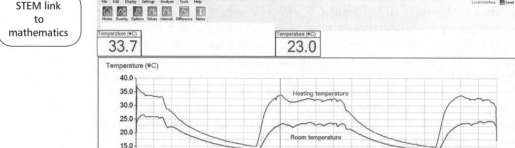

Figure 4.5   A graph of radiator and room temperature over two days

 Reflective activity

Can you remember a science activity or event that prompted learners to ask many questions? What were they learning about? Was the activity hands-on? Would you say that the curiosity shown was down to the subject matter, the activity or a combination of both?

Figure 4.6   Partial solar eclipse

The partial solar eclipse in March 2015 was a time when many learners asked questions about science. They may have been curious specifically about what was happening to the Sun but the general increase in interest about space may have led to wider questions about planets, aliens or black holes. The depth of curiosity here was undoubtedly, at least in part, due to it being an event that learners witnessed for themselves, enhanced no doubt by media coverage and special eclipse-related activities in schools.

Curiosity in a classroom – an informal study

Loewenstein's model of curiosity would seem to predict that learners will not be curious about things they know nothing about (Loewenstein, 1994). In an attempt to test this theory a questionnaire was devised for learners in which they were asked to say which of several questions they were most curious about. The learners had to identify two questions they were curious about from the following six.

1.   What is adrenaline?

2.   What is DNA?

These two questions were chosen as it was thought that learners would recognise the terms and would be able to link them to the recently completed science topic about the human body. It was predicted that these were the questions in which learners would be most curious; they already held a strong mental model about the human body and these questions would have exposed gaps in their knowledge they should want to fill.

3. What is ultraviolet light?

4. What is a light wave?

These questions were chosen to fit with the learners' new science topic on light, which they had only recently started. The prediction was that they would not be as curious about these as they would know less about the topic.

5. What is chromatography?

6. What is an aerogel?

The final two questions were designed to be on topics about which, it was hoped, the learners knew nothing. It was predicted that they might therefore show little or no curiosity in these. Which pair of questions would you predict learners would be most curious about?

The questionnaire was completed by learners from Year 5 and 6 with a range of attainment. The results were surprising. Fifteen out of twenty children said they were curious about either question five or question six. In contrast, only seven out of twenty showed any curiosity about either question one or question two. Eight out of twenty learners said they were curious about both question five and six. Only five learners said they were not curious about question five or six (see Figure 4.7).

Learners were significantly more curious about questions 5 and 6 than predicted by the author. Perhaps these results show that curiosity is a more complex phenomenon than Loewenstein's model would suggest. The results appear to support Litman's compromising model, which suggests that the drive theories of Freud and others, Piaget's Violation of Expectations theory and Loewenstein's model all play a significant role in our curiosity (Litman, 2005; Freud, 2015; Loewenstein, 1994). The learners here show a definite curiosity for subjects about which they know nothing. However, it is important to remember that this was only an informal study with a tiny sample size and, even in asking questions five and six, something is revealed about the subject even if it is only the name. The learners were asked to

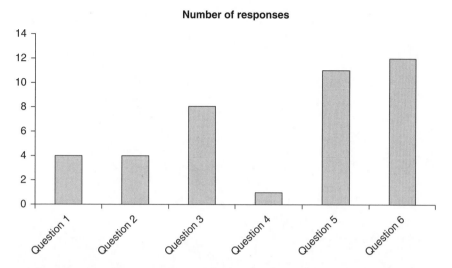

Figure 4.7   Which questions were learners curious about?

record the reasons for their choices and these were sometimes revealing.

Reasons why learners were curious about chromatography:

'I don't know what chromatography is.'

'It sounds very hard working and serious.'

'I think it is interesting because of 'ography' at the end like 'photography.''

The last learner above is clearly making links with other learning and seeing where this new information might fit within their previous knowledge. The examples below reveal true interest in the unknown.

Reasons why learners were curious about aerogel:

'Because I don't know what it means.'

'I want to know what an aerogel is.'

'No clue, so excited to find out, and curious.'

'I have never heard of this and would like to look up some more about this.'

Figure 4.8   The refraction of light makes this pencil appear bent or broken

Does curiosity need to be managed? Dealing with levels of understanding

Curiosity is clearly a powerful tool for science so surely the most curious people would make the best scientists? Here we find a paradox. When trying to understand scientific concepts, the people who are the most curious sometimes appear to struggle.

Try this now: Place a pencil into a glass half full of water.

You will see that the pencil looks broken where it emerges from the water and it may also look slightly wider in the water. This observation may lead you to seek an explanation (see Figure 4.8.).

The following questions represent levels of complexity and abstraction. In primary science we might just use questions one and two but the later questions show how a line of questioning can lead to deeper reasoning and complication.

Question 1: Why does the pencil look bent?

It is because the direction of the reflected light from the pencil changes as it moves from the water into the glass, then into the air. Some people might just accept this. But what if you are curious? Does the light really change direction or is the pencil actually broken?

Put your fingers into the water to feel the pencil. It doesn't feel bigger in the water and now your fingers look bent too! But why does the light change direction? Water, glass and air are all transparent so light just goes through them. Doesn't it?

Question 2: Why does the light change direction (refract)?

To understand why light changes direction as it crosses from one transparent material to another is tricky. We first have to understand that the speed of light is different in different materials.

Question 3: Why is the speed of light different in different materials?

The denser the material the slower light can move through it. That probably feels like an acceptable fact because it fits with other more familiar situations, it can be much slower to move through a crowded shop than an empty one. Thick syrup pours more slowly than less viscous water. These analogies allow us to link the information we have just learned with other information already held in our brain. This makes it 'feel' acceptable; it is not counter-intuitive.

So now back to **Question 2**: Why does the light change direction?

To explain why these different speeds of light cause a change of direction we can use the analogy of a tractor moving from a road, where it can travel quite fast, on to a muddy field, where it moves more slowly. As the tractor comes off the road the wheels slip slightly in the mud causing slower travel. So, as the tractor turns off the road, the wheels on the right hit the mud first. This causes the right side of the tractor to slow down before the left side causing the tractor to turn slightly. Light is a little like that, which is all very well if we accept it. But what if we are unhappy to accept this explanation because we are still curious about some of those steps? This could lead to question 4.

Question 4: Why does light travel more slowly in denser materials?

So now it's getting really hard. We have to understand the interactions between the photons of light and the molecules of the material it is passing through. And if we ask 'why' again we are easily into the realm of complex quantum physics.

The difficulty is that you need a great deal of extra information to understand each level of the answer. So here lies the paradox. Within the education system, those who do well at science are often those who curtail their curiosity and accept the first level of answer without further question. The pencil looks bent because the light bends.

The advantage of knowing when to curtail your curiosity is that it gives you time to assimilate the knowledge, to see the effect in other situations, in spectacles, a magnifying glass, and to link it with other analogous areas of knowledge in your brain. Then, later, when the knowledge is secure, you are ready to challenge it and ask why. Asking why too soon might have the same effect as trying to run before you can walk. Perhaps ideas and concepts, like skills, need practice and only when they are secure can we go on and deal with more complex notions. As teachers, we can provide learners with a range of analogies to help secure their learning. While we celebrate the asking of complex questions by learners, we should be explicit about when a question goes beyond what we can reasonably expect to understand at any given stage.

As teachers, we can help learners develop their curiosity. We can look out for times when learners are going too fast and need to spend a little time reinforcing their understanding before moving on. At these times we can provide activities that allow children to demonstrate, model and explain the new learning; a class who have been exploring how the different poles of magnets behave can usefully create a physical dance or game where they re-create the actions of the different poles; learners who have been finding out about the ways light changes direction can draw diagrams to show how the eye or a periscope works. A particularly useful technique in primary school is modelling a phenomenon physically, using role-play or dance. This can be done in class, in the school hall or even in the playground (Cross and Board, 2014). Computer modelling is another useful tool and, unlike role-play, is used by scientists to answer questions and to explore and develop ideas. In the primary classroom it can be used to reinforce learning by modelling phenomena.

Curiosity and modelling

After researching the orbits of the Earth and Moon, learners in Year 5 were encouraged to explore different ways of modelling this. Two-dimensional card models were created and physical models involving different-sized balls were used before the children were asked 'How can we model this using a computer?' The children were initially set a computational thinking task of evaluating the pros and cons of different software and deciding how each might be programmed to create the model. Working in pairs they used their chosen application and were very curious to see how they could make the different bodies follow the correct paths. The learners chose from a range of software including stop-frame animation in Pivot (http://pivot-stickfigure-animator.en.uptodown.com), programming using Scratch (https://scratch.mit.edu) and using custom animations in Microsoft Power Point (see Figure 4.9). Throughout the activities

STEM link
to computing

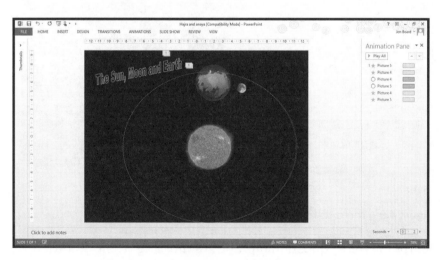

Power Point

Figure 4.9 *(Continued)*

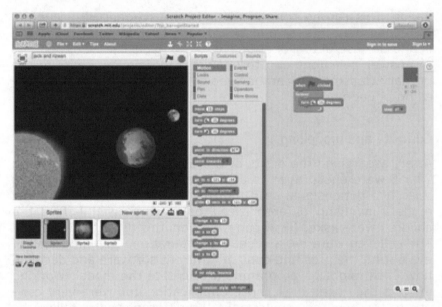

STEM link
to computing

Scratch

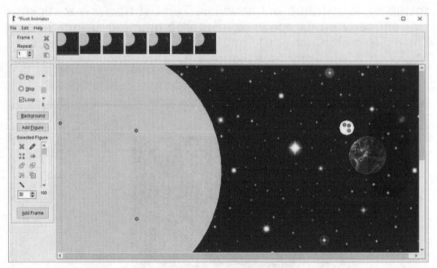

Pivot

Figure 4.9   Three different ways to model orbits

learners were questioning and reinforcing their knowledge,
'Does the Earth or the Moon move faster?', 'How far away
should we put the Sun?' Learners were still curious but exploring within their understanding rather than beyond.

A scientifically curious classroom

Science is based on questions so it follows that a scientifically curious classroom should exploit questions in every form. The most powerful questions being those elicited from curious learners. These learners will be beginning to appreciate the power of science to address questions we have about the world. Some questions can be answered by a test; others by a larger investigation and some may occupy us for a lifetime.

 Reflective activity

Consider these questions, which can be dealt with by a test, which will require sustained investigation and research:

- *Which of these objects float?*
- *Is there life in outer space?*
- *What are the best conditions for growth of sunflower seedlings?*
- *Which diet is the best for my health?*
- *What materials keep me warmest?*
- *Can planet Earth support high-energy consumption by each of what soon will be a human population of 9 billion?*

As teachers, we need to develop our skills and knowledge about the very best ways to enable learners as confident science question posers and answer seekers.

Conclusion

Curiosity is a powerful tool, which can have a very positive impact on classroom science; however, it needs to be managed. As teachers, we need to understand its power and its consequences. Used reflectively, curiosity can open up new and interesting areas of science. We have seen how the curiosity of scientists has led to groundbreaking discoveries and how curiosity is an integral part of the process of science enquiry. The next chapter will explore how teachers can develop learners' curiosity within the enquiry process and examine further techniques for promoting healthy curiosity within primary science and across the STEM subjects.

Chapter summary

Having read this chapter you will:

- be aware of the fundamental nature of curiosity within science;
- have reflected on how curiosity needs to be encouraged and managed;
- be aware of some strategies for managing and developing curiosity.

CHAPTER 5

WAYS TO ENHANCE CURIOSITY IN PRIMARY SCIENCE

Chapter objectives

After reading this chapter you will:

- recognise techniques for raising science questions with learners;
- find out how elicitation and predictions develop learners' curiosity in science;
- appreciate that increasing learner autonomy in science can increase curiosity.

Overview

We saw in the previous chapter how curiosity can be the trigger that begins the process of scientific enquiry. Chapter 4 also noted how curiosity is an important factor in other parts of the scientific process. This chapter will seek to explain the importance of some of the stages we follow in an investigation. From making predictions to making conclusions, curiosity can be a powerful driver. There are many effective techniques that can be used in primary science lessons to develop curiosity. Some of these will be familiar as they are already used in classrooms but this chapter aims to analyse these techniques and examine how their potential for developing curiosity can be maximised.

Promoting curiosity in primary science

In primary science lessons, curious learners can be observed showing great engagement in their learning. They might be asking questions, making predictions or taking careful and accurate measurements, but is it their curiosity that leads them to act in this way or is it this kind of action that makes them curious in the first place? The answer is probably that it is a combination of both but, in practising the skills and techniques of curious scientists and having time for focused discussion, the curiosity of many learners does appear to grow.

Promoting curiosity in science is ...?

This section considers pedagogical approaches that can help to cultivate and maintain levels of curiosity in science.

Curiosity in science is ... about asking questions

Try asking a 'why' question now. If you know the answer, question it again with 'why'. Repeat this just a few times and you will quickly reach the boundaries of current scientific understanding. With the right stimulus it is easy for primary-aged children to ask such questions. Quite an achievement for a nine-year-old to ask for knowledge that nobody yet knows! Perhaps finding answers could become their life's work?

Curiosity may launch the scientific process but where does the initial question come from? In many classrooms the question is set by the teacher, determined as part of the planning for the lesson. However, there are more creative ways to arrive at an enquiry question, approaches which will develop curiosity. Asking learners to create their own questions is a powerful way of fostering curiosity and many of the questions they come up with can be answered through practical enquiry activities. But how can teachers ensure that learners are curious enough to be able to come up with their own questions?

Allowing children the opportunity to explore or observe an object or phenomena creates an opportunity for curiosity. Even observing familiar objects, such as snails or magnets, within the context of a science lesson encourages learners, directed by the teacher, to observe new details or to play with phenomena in new ways. This can lead to a sense of awe and wonder from which questions can be generated. Curiosity is a powerful feeling, but it is often only a general sense of wanting to find out more.

Scientific questions crystallise this general feeling and signpost the direction in which to hunt for answers.

It is straightforward to create these exploration activities and they fit well at the beginning of a new section of science work. Explorations are also a useful technique for the elicitation of learners' understanding. Five minutes with a magnifying glass and a selection of rocks is plenty of time for Year 3 learners to begin to ask what rocks are made from, what the shiny bits are and whether they are very valuable. Ten minutes with magnets and a challenge to see what they can find out will probably establish that two red ends and two blue ends push apart, one of each colour pull together, they stick to metal and that they work through paper. But there will also be questions (see Figure 5.1). Why are they attracted to this metal but not this one? Which is the strongest magnet? How do they work? Some of these questions will have answers that are too complex for primary

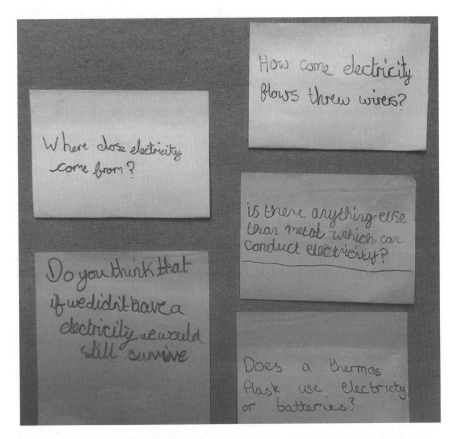

Figure 5.1 Learners' questions about electricity

classrooms but the questions themselves are still valuable and should be collected and prized, perhaps displayed. An 'I wonder...' wall or a poster of 'Great Unanswered Questions' would be a curiosity-raising addition to any science display, especially when supported by the promise of a reward for any plausible answers researched at home. This has the added benefit of encouraging learning beyond the classroom, creating further opportunities for curiosity to develop.

Learners' curiosity will be engaged when they witness adults and other learners asking questions that they clearly do not know the answer to. 'I wonder whether...?' 'I wonder how...?' In fact, perhaps wondering is one of the keys to curiosity because it can be infectious. Questions could be considered a symptom of curiosity, and a discussion about the questions of some learners can have the effect of infecting others with the curiosity bug.

Sticky note questions

Asking learners to record their questions on sticky notes means that each question becomes a separate movable entity. This creates several useful learning opportunities. Learners can be asked to classify the questions, sorting them into groups. The groups could be based around the subjects of different questions or other ways such as how they could be investigated, by using a fair test or by research using secondary sources, for example. Sticky note questions can be displayed around the classroom in different ways such as on a pair of posters of answered and unanswered questions. Questions from the beginning of a topic can be kept and then looked at again towards the end. Incorporating the questions into a sticky note mind map of what has been learnt is an excellent way for learners to review their learning.

STEM link to mathematics

CASE STUDY

Exploring snails

As part of work on local habitats, each table of Year 2 learners was presented with three snails in the middle of a shallow tray (see Figure 5.2).

The learners had magnifying glasses to make detailed observations and to give a focus to this exploration activity. At first the snails were still and hid in their shells (snails often do this in a dry, noisy environment) but as the learners became quiet and a little water was sprinkled on to each tray the snails emerged and began to explore. This caused great excitement in the learners, as they were able to observe the snails' bodies and antennae closely. They were curious to see what would happen when the snails reached the edge of each tray and some were surprised to see the snails carry on moving straight up a vertical wall.

Figure 5.2 Year 2 exploration with snails

Next came the opportunity, for those who wanted to, to lift the snails and place them back into the centre of the tray. This allowed learners to observe the underside of the snail and see how the snail reacted by pulling itself back towards its shell. The questions that came from this activity meant that the class could build on their own curiosity in the following lessons.

(Continued)

(Continued)

- What do snails eat?
- How do they move?
- How far do they travel?
- Do they spend more time here or there, e.g. in light or dark?
- Why do they leave slime?
- Why are they slow?
- Why do they have a shell?

The example above is one where questions help to drive the curiosity and the science. The questions raised led to work on how snails survive in their habitat, snail predators, snails' diet and food chains. The learners made the link between snails and tortoises; both can afford to be slow because they carry protection from predators. There is no need to move fast when you can hide inside your shell.

Perhaps this process of exploration and sharing questions raises levels of curiosity because it appears to fit with Loewenstein's reference point model (Loewenstein, 1994). Loewenstein explains curiosity as the result of an information gap, of realising that there is something that can be known but is not. The exploration activity allows learners to isolate details and phenomena, and question their own understanding of them. Where understanding is found to be lacking, curiosity, grows.

However, these early questions have to be carefully managed by the teacher. A teacher who gives answers too readily may extinguish the curiosity of a learner. A learner who shows curiosity with a question such as 'Eeugh, what's that bug?' and is quickly supplied the answer that it is a shield bug, may find their curiosity satisfied so promptly that they feel perhaps there is nothing more to find out; their interest quickly dies away. So, as teachers interested in facilitating learning rather than supplying knowledge, we need to give curiosity time and space to grow. Let the questions multiply before even beginning the search to find answers. 'How many legs does it have?' 'Are those things eyes?' 'Can it fly?' Once learners are sufficiently interested and engaged, providing the name of the creature may not have such a negative effect as the learners' interest is now focused on finding out the answers to their other questions about this 'shield bug'.

Curiosity in science is ... about making use of elicitation

Elicitation is a useful technique that is frequently used at the beginning of a section of work to find out what learners already know about a specific area of learning. This is clearly useful for the teacher in that it helps to identify what learners already know, what they have not yet learned and, importantly, any misconceptions they might have. Before examining the role that misconceptions can play in generating curiosity, it is worth considering the benefits of elicitation from a learner's perspective.

Elicitation activities are meta-cognitive as they enable learners to explore their own knowledge and understanding. As part of this self-evaluation process they have to remember their knowledge of a subject, and they will sometimes realise that their memories are somewhat rusty.

A less than perfect, 'patchy', memory is part of being human and is the reason we often revisit subjects within a spiral curriculum. The more we repeat and extend the same topics in different ways or contexts, the more the learning is reused and reinforced, establishing more secure and much less patchy memories. Interestingly, primary science in the National Curriculum published in 2013 (DfE, 2013) has lost the spiral structure that was present within the previous curriculum. This is, at least in part, due to the removal of most physics topics from Key Stage One. However, in order to retain a spiral curriculum, some schools are still teaching some physics topics at Year 1 and 2.

These 'patchy' memories are a common cause of curiosity. Having discovered gaps in their understanding, learners are often keen to fill in those gaps with knowledge. This is an example of Loewenstein's reference point model of curiosity (Loewenstein, 1994); we have previously referred to this as the jigsaw model. Curiosity is the drive to find missing pieces, to complete, or at least see more detail, of the picture. As Donald Rumsfeld, the former U.S Secretary of State for Defence put it:

'We know, there are known knowns; there are things we know we know. We also know there are known unknowns; that is to say we know there are some things we do not know. But there are also unknown unknowns, the ones we don't know we don't know (U.S. Department of Defense, 2002).'

Although initially confusing, this is a very helpful reference. In terms of curiosity, Loewenstein is simply saying that there is a drive to turn known unknowns into known knowns. This is supported to some extent by Vygotsky's zone of proximal development (Vygotsky, 1978). This theory states that there is a blurred area between what a learner can do independently and what they cannot do at all. This is the zone of proximal development where a learner can only operate with the support of a capable other. Learners working in this zone will be dealing with their known unknowns. Therefore, this is the area of learning in which they are mostly likely, at least in theory, to be curious about. However, the informal study about children's curiosity about six science questions in Chapter 4 shows that some learners, at least, have a curiosity about unknown unknowns; a helpful challenge perhaps to the theoretical ideas above. Perhaps the teacher's job is to help reveal unknown unknowns so that they become known unknowns and so contexts for curiosity.

There is another aspect of elicitation worth mentioning; this is the impact of shared learning. Elicitation activities are often highly productive and motivating when they are group activities that involve discussion. Here learners can reflect on their own understanding and compare it to that of others. Often a mismatch is exposed, bringing an unknown unknown into the known unknown category. This perhaps exposes curiosity as a driver of social constructivism, the notion that collective activity allows learners to achieve more than when working alone (Vygotsky, 1978). Clearly, this type of experience can create curiosity in learners who become aware that others appear to know or understand more than they do themselves. But it can also be significant for those whose understanding appears the most complete. These learners can be in a position of having to explain their knowledge and having their mental model questioned. Most people are familiar with the situation where you feel that you understand something only to find that you struggle when trying to explain it to others. The questioning and explanation challenges understanding and the inevitable search for effective analogies will develop and strengthen mental models.

Elicitation strategies

Elicitation techniques that involve discussion between learners tend to be effective in exposing misconceptions and gaps in our knowledge and understanding. Here are some useful strategies.

- Statements
  Statements that are often true but not always, such as 'Solids are hard', encourage learners to recall and discuss examples of

when the statement is not true. Asking learners to state whether they agree or disagree and to say why tends to work well.

- Concept cartoons

   These are simple drawings of children making different, often contradictory statements about a scientific phenomenon. Again, learners can state reasons why they might agree or disagree with the different statements or they can improve the statements to make them more accurate (Naylor and Keogh, 2000).

- Sticky note mind maps

   Setting groups of learners the challenge of creating a shared mind map that shows what they understand about a topic creates a situation where they have to discuss how different ideas fits together. Using sticky notes allows learners to reorganise the structure they are creating at any time, leading to more open discussion and more flexible thinking.

Elicitation activities that involve sharing and discussion of ideas are likely to create curiosity through two distinct mechanisms: Loewenstein's self-identification of a knowledge gap (Loewenstein, 1994) and social constructivism's revelations of mismatches in understanding across a peer group. These mismatches have clear links with Piaget's violated expectations model of curiosity (Loewenstein, 1994). This model suggests that curiosity stems from an interest in the differences between what we expect and what actually happens (see Chapter 3 on disequilibrium (Piaget, 1958). So when a learner shares their understanding of a topic and discovers that others have a different interpretation or simply know more, there is a 'violation of expectations', which they become curious to resolve.

Curiosity in Science is ... about recognising and using misconceptions

One of the purposes of elicitation is in revealing misconceptions that learners may hold. Once made explicit, these misconceptions provide an excellent breeding ground for curiosity. The disturbing feeling, 'Well if it's not what I thought, then what on earth is it?' can be a strong motivator. Scientific misconceptions fit directly with Piaget's violation of expectations model of curiosity (Loewenstein, 1994).

CASE STUDY

Misconception about magnets

The learners in a Year 3 class were planning an investigation to discover which of a collection of magnets was the strongest. Most of the groups planned to test the magnets by counting how many paper clips a magnet would pick up or how many individual paper clips would attract together to make a chain when attached to each magnet. But, due to a misconception, one group planned to test which magnet could hold itself on to the metal radiator for the longest (see Figure 5.3). The misconception being that, like people, the magnets would get tired. After testing the magnets, and discovering that they did not suffer from a lack of endurance, the learners were keen to discuss why people get tired but magnets do not. This led to them doing some independent reading about how muscles need oxygen from the blood to function.

STEM link
to
mathematics

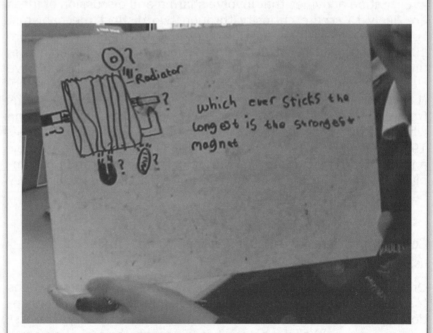

Figure 5.3 A misconception about magnets

Curiosity in science is ... about exploiting skill development

Predictions

Predictions can have a similar curiosity-enhancing effect to elicitation in that they can be used to encourage metacognition. But this will only happen if learners have to give explicit reasons for their predictions. This forces learners to self-evaluate and to reflect on their understanding. As before, this creates curiosity due to the learners' desire to see whether their predicted piece of the picture will be correct and fit with the rest of their mental jigsaw. However, learners should be encouraged to understand that a good prediction is not one that turns out to be correct, but one that is based on evidence. In fact, the most interesting predictions are often those that turn out to be wrong. This is because they show either that there is something incorrect in the learner's initial understanding or that there were unknown unknowns, which have just become known unknowns. Both of these outcomes tend to increase learners' curiosity; the former is a clear case of Piaget's violation of expectations, the latter of Loewenstein's reference point model (Loewenstein, 1994).

CASE STUDY

Thermal insulators

An example that combines the effective use of predictions with knowledge of common misconceptions can be seen in this case study of two consecutive lessons in Year 4. In the first lesson the learners were guided in planning an experiment to investigate which fabrics would keep bottles of warm water warm. The investigation involved choosing a material that they predicted would work well and one that they predicted would not and then testing both (see Figure 5.4). The learners predicted correctly that thicker fabrics would insulate the warm water well and that thinner fabrics would not.

The second lesson required learners to work with less support on a similar investigation but this time into which fabrics would keep cold water cold. The learners were astonished to discover that the thick

(Continued)

STEM link to mathematics

STEM link to design and technology

(Continued)

fabrics, that they predicted would warm the water, were again the most effective insulators. Owing to a massive violation of expectations the investigation led to much curiosity about how insulators work, what heat is and whether warm coats really are warm.

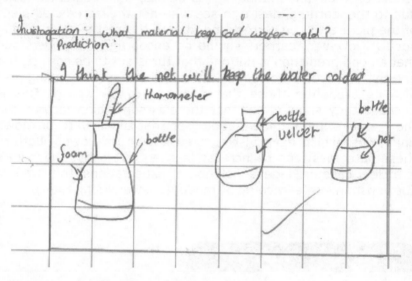

Figure 5.4 Prediction about thermal conductors

STEM link to mathematics

Results

It was noted in Chapter 4 that one of the key areas of science enquiry that creates curiosity is the process of forming conclusions based on results. This can be used to a teacher's advantage if work is carefully planned so that the questions that stem from the results of one investigation lead into the next part of the topic that needs to be covered. It may seem that planning like this would be time-consuming but in fact it is often as simple as teaching a topic backwards. Teachers often plan lessons so that learners can take small steps, gaining understanding along the way until they have made significant progress in their knowledge or skills. But reversing this process allows curiosity to develop and is therefore more motivating for learners. Consider the example of learning about the internal organs of the human body with Year 6. A logical approach would be to teach about the function of the cardiovascular system, the digestive system, bones and muscles and then to link these up by creating a diagram of the human body. But teaching it backwards creates greater opportunity for curiosity. Start by asking learners to create a 3D life-size paper model of a human body and provide them with materials for research and they will happily model what they know until their curiosity leads them to research new information and ask specific questions about function (see Figure 5.5). The subsequent lessons now become opportunities to answer questions asked by learners:

- What does the intestine do?
- Why does the heart have two sides?
- What is a trachea?

The learners' curiosity is now driving their learning.

Another example using the same technique is in planning for a series of lessons about the life cycle of a flowering plant. Clearly, with a cycle you could begin anywhere but it can be very productive to start at what might be considered the end, with the fruit.

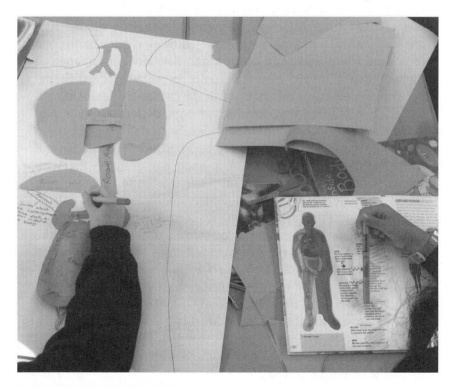

Figure 5.5 Curious about the body

So the first lesson can be exploring or even hunting for the fruits of different plants such as blackberries, rosehips, sycamore helicopters and, best of all, Himalayan balsam that has pods which explode when touched. Dissecting the fruits to find the seeds inside tends to lead to questions about seed dispersal. Fruits with the remains of flower parts such as sepals or stamen still visible often get learners wondering whether the fruit has something to do with the flower. This then leads into a series of lessons, each of which explores the questions of the previous lesson, covering the parts of the flower and pollination, until we get back to conditions under which a plant will germinate from a seed in the first place.

CASE STUDY

Teaching circuits by making electrical buggies

STEM link
to design and
technology

A series of science lessons with Years 5 and 6 on electrical circuits was planned to coincide with a design technology project that involved making a moving buggy powered by an electric motor. The links were made explicit to learners and they were encouraged to discover how different electrical components behaved when the polarity of the battery was reversed in the circuit. The learners' curiosity to find out how they could improve the designs for their buggies meant they could quickly see that by reversing the batteries they could make their buggies move backwards or forwards. Several switch designs were trialled before a simple pair of flaps with metal foil partly insulated with sticky tape was established as a working model (see Figure 5.6). With the battery connected to one side of the switch and the motor, via long wires, to the other, a flap with two parallel foil strips allowed for forward movement while the other flap with crossed but insulated foil strips reversed the motor. Throughout this process the learners encountered many problems with the switch design and construction, mainly in connection with positioning the insulating sticky tape and the conducting paper fasteners correctly. But all of these difficulties were overcome by the learners' curiosity and in the process they learnt more about electrical circuits, conductivity and switch design (also see buggy activities in Chapter 7 on computing).

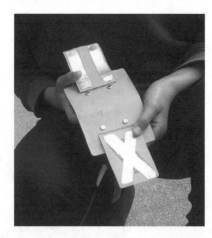

Figure 5.6   Child showing a forward and reverse switch for a buggy

Curiosity in Science is ... about learners being scientists

In a science investigation, one of the most important factors that determines the degree of learners' curiosity is the extent to which they feel they are in control. Do they have the opportunity to set the question, to plan or change the investigation to satisfy their curiosity or are they simply following instructions? Increasing the independence of learners, or 'putting them in the driving seat', allows creativity, curiosity and motivation to flourish (Cross and Board, 2014). The question for teachers is how to achieve this. In a primary classroom with, often, more than 30 learners and no easy access to science equipment, how can we facilitate learners planning and developing their own enquiries? The solution lies in doing things step by step, introducing independence a little at a time. For example, a Year 2 class who were investigating sound were curious about why some animals had very large ears. This led to the teacher planning an investigation where learners made their own 'big ears' and used them to listen to quiet sounds (see Figure 5.7). Rather than the teacher deciding which sounds the learners should listen to, the learners were allowed to explore the classroom freely looking for sound sources that interested them. Even this small degree of independence encouraged the learners to be curious. They shared their different results and encouraged each other to listen to the sounds they had discovered.

To achieve greater independence for learners, a topic could be started with a series of activities that generate questions, such

Figure 5.7 Using a 'big ear' to listen to quiet sounds

as exploration, elicitation and making predictions. Learners can then identify the questions that they could investigate and the teacher can introduce a degree of choice into the investigations that follow. This way we can maximise learners' initial curiosity and then design the investigation process to allow that curiosity to grow.

There are two distinct types of investigation that allow learners a degree of independence. The first type is an investigation where the teacher chooses the variable to be changed but learners can choose how they change that variable. Here the equipment and method tend to be the same for all learners but the choice of how to change the variable allows individuals to pursue their own curiosity. An example would be the investigation mentioned above where learners investigate the thermal insulation properties of different fabrics. Here, the procedure is the same for every group but there is a choice of which fabrics to test. This only provides for a small degree of independence but it is enough to engage learners due to their curiosity in the performance of their chosen fabrics compared to the choices of others.

The second type allows learners a greater degree of control. Here they choose which variable they will change and their choice

STEM link
to design and
technology

will determine the procedure and the equipment required. In this situation, even though the whole class may be investigating different aspects of the same question, each group would need to plan their own investigation in detail. For example, an investigation into which factors make a paper towel dry more quickly: here, learners can choose to investigate whether heat, wind, surface area or any other factor affects the rate at which a paper towel dries. Groups who chose different variables would need to plan and complete different investigations with different equipment. However, there is still plenty of common ground; all learners would need to make sure that they control the variables they are not investigating to make their test fair. Also, each group would need to use a 'control' to make a comparison. So learners investigating whether wind speeds up evaporation would need to compare a drying paper towel hung in front of a fan with another in identical conditions except that it is well away from the wind. A recent investigation of this type led to some learners predicting that since sound is vibrations in the air, then perhaps it would speed up evaporation. They compared a wet paper towel hung up in a noisy room with one in a quiet room and concluded that as far as they could measure it made no difference. This was a far more effective investigation than one into whether heat made a difference; here the curiosities of the learners led them to find out new information rather than confirming what they already knew.

CASE STUDY

What makes food go mouldy?

Here learners have a choice of how to change a set variable.

As part of a topic on micro-organisms, curious learners in Years 5 and 6 asked the question 'What makes food go mouldy?' (see Figure 5.8). This quickly developed into a range of questions from the learners:

Do bananas make other food go mouldy faster?

Does cola make food rot?

Does dirty food rot faster than clean food?

STEM link to design and technology

(Continued)

(Continued)

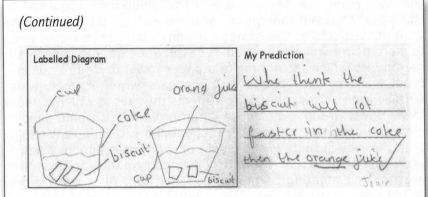

| Labelled Diagram | My Prediction |

Labelled Diagram text: cup, orang juic, coke, biscuit, cup, biscuit

My Prediction: We think the biscut will rot faster in the coke then the orange juie

Jime

Figure 5.8 A prediction about mould

An investigation was planned into mouldy food where learners could choose which types of food they used in order to satisfy their own curiosity. Cleanliness in the form of 'dirt', or soil, and antibacterial hand gel, was introduced as a second variable to allow greater flexibility. Investigations into whether bananas make oranges go mouldy more quickly (see Figure 5.9) and whether dirty cheese goes mouldy sooner than clean cheese reinforced learners' understanding of food hygiene and micro-organism growth, but learners were very surprised to discover that cola seemed to prevent food from going mouldy. All learners expected the opposite and the reasons given for their predictions showed that this was because they knew that sweet drinks rot your teeth. They were then very curious to find out that the sugar is food for bacteria in your mouth and it is the acidic waste from these bacteria that causes tooth decay. This is a clear example of effective learning taking place when predictions are found to be incorrect. The investigation

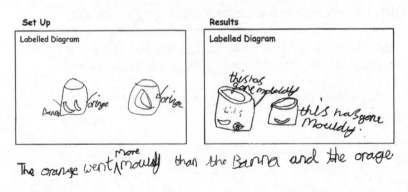

Set Up — Labelled Diagram: banana, orange, orange

Results — Labelled Diagram: this has gone moldly, this, this has gone mouldy.

The orange went more mouldy than the Banna and the orage

Figure 5.9 Do bananas make other food go mouldy faster?

developed the learners' curiosity yet was simple to manage; the only equipment required was clear pots with lids, labels, soil, hand gel and a selection of food.

Safety Note: Use sealed containers to ensure learners do not inhale spores from mouldy food.

CASE STUDY

What affects your heart rate?

Here learners have a choice of which variable to investigate.

After investigating the effects of exercise, Year 6 learners were asked to plan an investigation into other factors that might affect heart rate. The previous investigation into exercise had taught them the skills needed to take their own pulse and had modelled a procedure that could be modified for the new investigation. This procedure had been presented as a simple algorithm for planning a fair test; change one thing, measure one thing, keep the rest the same. The learners were encouraged to use this algorithm when planning their own investigation.

STEM link to mathematics

STEM link to computing

Fair Testing as an Algorithm

Change one thing

Measure one thing

Keep the rest the same

The learners were curious about chocolate and coffee, as they had heard that these could increase heart rate and this initial curiosity soon widened into questions about being scared or bored and the effects of holding your breath.

- Does being cold decrease your heart rate?
- Does your heart rate increase when someone pops a balloon?
- Does reading a scary book increase your heart rate?

(Continued)

(Continued)

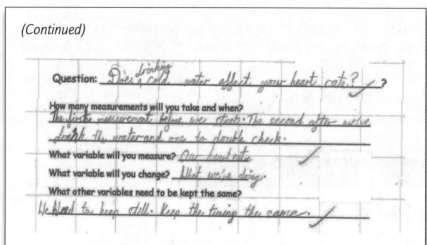

Figure 5.10 Independent investigation planning

STEM link
to
mathematics

Groups of learners used the algorithm to plan their own investigation and decide what measurements to take and when (see Figure 5.10). The learners were very curious about the findings of other groups, which made the presentation of results to the class a meaningful exercise. Many learners were curious to understand the reason why being scared or startled increases your heart rate which led to research about the human 'flight or flight' reaction.

Conclusion

While curiosity is enhanced and developed through all subjects, science brings a whole world of exploration and investigation through which personal curiosity can be pursued. It is reasonable to assume that learners who leave primary school with a real curiosity about the world and specifically science will have a greater chance of success in science and other subjects. One of the key roles of a primary teacher, therefore, is to enable and encourage curiosity in the learners they teach. The approaches described above can achieve this.

There is a further benefit of encouraging curiosity in learners that has not yet been mentioned: the benefit gained by the teacher. Curious learners are inherently more motivated and usually more enthusiastic. Most teachers would agree that learners who are switched on and excited about the subject are more enjoyable to teach. Developing learners' curiosity therefore has numerous advantageous spin-offs.

Chapter summary

Having read this chapter you will:

- be familiar with the power of pupil questions in science;
- understand how elicitation activities and predictions can develop curiosity;
- be aware of the link between choices that promote independence and curiosity.

CHAPTER 6

CURIOUS LEARNERS IN PRIMARY COMPUTING

OLDER PEOPLE SIT DOWN AND ASK, 'WHAT IS IT?' BUT THE BOY ASKS, 'WHAT CAN I DO WITH IT?'

STEVE JOBS

Chapter objectives

After reading this chapter you will:

- know about the role curiosity has played in significant technological innovations;
- have a developing understanding of the skills in computing which enhance and utilise curiosity;
- have a developing understanding of the features of a computing curious classroom.

Overview

This chapter will look at the relevance of curiosity in educational computing. It will start by exploring the content of the English computing curriculum (DfE, 2013), looking at how it breaks down into computer science, information technology and digital literacy. It will look at incredible innovations which have changed the world as a result of individuals exercising their curious minds in the context of computing. It will also explore the skills in computing which are linked to, and enable, learners' curiosity. Finally, we will consider the features of a computing curious classroom. In the next chapter we present a series of case studies which explain in more detail how we develop curiosity in primary computing.

To help ensure schools' curriculum keeps pace with our technology-rich world, September 2014 saw the introduction of a new subject in the National Curriculum, computing, to replace information and communication technology (ICT) (DfEE/QCA,1999). The ICT curriculum was deemed by many professional bodies as outdated, uninspiring and not fit for purpose. Publications, such as *Shutdown or restart?* (Royal Society, 2012) and *Next Gen.* (Livingstone and Hope (Nesta), 2011) called for change. The main failing of the ICT curriculum, as pointed out in these reports, was too great a focus on solely developing ICT skills, that is, teaching learners to be competent users of software such as word processing, presentation and database packages. While such skills are undoubtedly important, so too are the skills in being creators of technology, by learning the computer science behind how to program for example. Both the Nesta (Livingstone and Hope, 2011) and The Royal Society (2012) reports found these to be the skills in demand by the world's growing digital technology economies. These were the skills that the valuable British computer games industry, for example, required from new recruits, and were struggling to find in young people who had received an 'ICT education'. These are the skills young learners need to be active participants in an ever more technology-driven world (Rushkoff, 2011). In Rushkoff's words, 'Program or be programmed.'

It followed that Nesta (2011) and The Royal Society (2012), along with groups such as Computing at School (www.computingatschool.org.uk), called for an increase of computer science within schools' curriculum. This opinion was also voiced by the Chairman of Google, Eric Schmidt, who in 2011 gave his MacTaggart Lecture in Edinburgh in which he explained: 'I was flabbergasted to learn that today computer science isn't even taught as standard in UK schools' and added that as the country which invented the computer we were 'throwing away [our] great computing heritage'. The government was quick to respond, and in January 2012 announced the disapplication of the ICT curriculum. The task of creating a new curriculum fell to the British Computer Society and the Royal Academy of Engineering who developed 'computing', which was introduced in September 2014 (DfE, 2013).

The change from ICT to computing may be viewed as part evolution, part revolution. Computing is an umbrella term used to describe a three-part curriculum made up of computer science, information technology and digital literacy. These three components each promote and utilise curiosity. Table 6.1 shows how computing divides up into these strands, as explained in the Computing at School publication: *Computing in the National Curriculum – A Guide for Primary Teachers* (www.com putingatschool.org.uk/data/uploads/CASPrimaryComputing.pdf).

The revolution was the introduction of computer science (though this was not strictly new as ICT did include 'data and control'). It is within the computer science strand that learners are taught about information, computation and digital systems. They learn how to analyse problems in computational terms,

Table 6.1 Computing subject content divided into computer science, information technology and digital literacy.

	KS1	KS2
Computer Science	Understand what algorithms are; how they are implemented as programs on digital devices; and that programs execute by following precise and unambiguous instructions	Design, write and debug programs that accomplish specific goals, including controlling or simulating physical systems; solve problems by decomposing them into smaller parts
	Create and debug simple programs	Use sequence, selection and repetition in programs; work with variables and various forms of input and output
	Use logical reasoning to predict the behaviour of simple programs	Use logical reasoning to explain how some simple algorithms work and to detect and correct errors in algorithms and programs
		Understand computer networks including the Internet; how they can provide multiple services, such as the World Wide Web
		Appreciate how [search] results are selected and ranked

	KS1	KS2
Information Technology	Use technology purposefully to create, organise, store, manipulate and retrieve digital content	Use search technologies effectively

Select, use and combine a variety of software (including internet services) on a range of digital devices to design and create a range of programs, systems and content that accomplish given goals, including collecting, analysing, evaluating and presenting data and information |
| **Digital Literacy** | Recognise common uses of information technology beyond school

Use technology safely and respectfully, keeping personal information private; identify where to go for help and support when they have concerns about content or contact on the internet or other online technologies | Understand the opportunities [networks] offer for communication and collaboration

Be discerning in evaluating digital content

Use technology safely, respectfully and responsibly; recognise acceptable/ unacceptable behaviour; identify a range of ways to report concerns about content and contact |

drawing upon their computational thinking skills and gain experience of writing programs.

In terms of evolution, the introduction of computing gave schools an opportunity to update their information technology and digital literacy provision. Learners develop experience using a variety of technology within these strands, creating digital content such as videos, podcast, presentations or programs. Being 'digitally literate' arises as learners engage in the computing curriculum as a whole, as they become competent, confident and creative users of technology set to take their place in a digital world. This includes knowing how to use technology responsibly and safely, covered within the E-Safety aspect of digital literacy.

The focus of this and the following chapter will primarily be on developing learners' curiosity about the computer science strand of computing. Throughout the whole of this book links are made to opportunities for developing information technology and digital literacy within cross-curricular contexts.

What is computational thinking?

The opening line of the computing purpose of study states:

> *A high-quality computing education equips pupils to use computational thinking and creativity to understand and change the world* (DfE, 2013).

As teachers, we are curious about this subject and how learners might respond to it. Terms that are new to us raise interesting questions. For example, what is computational thinking?

Computational thinking is not thinking like a computer, as computers aren't capable of thought (Alan Turing felt this might change in the future, see below). Computational thinking describes a set of skills we can draw upon to solve a problem. If, for example, learners were challenged to program an invasion game about the Vikings, they would use computational thinking skills to design the game before they use a programming language, e.g. Scratch©, to code it. Barefoot Computing (www.barefootcas.org.uk) sets out six computational thinking concepts: logic, algorithms, decomposition, pattern, abstraction and evaluation, and five approaches: tinkering, creating, debugging, persevering and collaborating (see Figure 6.1).

In the Viking game example given above, it is likely learners will have broken down the problem into smaller more manageable tasks (decomposition). They would determine what information was and was not important to include (abstraction) and work out the steps and/or rules which describe the game (algorithms). It is our curiosity about how we will create the game which leads us to take these steps in its design. While this example results in writing a program, computational thinking isn't exclusively concerned with computing and computers. These general problem-solving skills can help learners across a wide range of subjects. For example, learners might work out the algorithm for conducting a scientific enquiry by decomposing the process into steps, or look out for patterns to help solve mathematical problems.

Figure 6.1 The Barefoot Computing Computational Thinker from www. barefootcas.org.uk

---

Reflective activity

Curious to learn more about computational thinking? Follow this link to sign up and access the Barefoot Computing resources http://barefootcas.org.uk

---

A computing pioneer: Alan Turing

We can foster learners' curiosity about computing by learning about early pioneers in this field, several of whom were British. Alan Turing is perhaps the best known. Turing (see Figure 6.2) was a pioneering British computer scientist and mathematician who is widely considered to be the father of theoretical computer science and artificial intelligence. Born in London on 23 June 1912, from a young age Turing was intensely curious about the scientific world around him. Archives of his teenage notebooks display an insatiable appetite for learning. Much of this study was self-directed, running far ahead of a constraining public school

STEM link to mathematics

Figure 6.2   Alan Turing memorial in Sackville Park, Manchester

syllabus which placed greater emphasis on the classics. Turing pursued his love of mathematics and science, and went on to study mathematics at King's College, Cambridge.

Turing is perhaps best remembered for his work leading the Hut 8 team at Bletchley Park, Britain's codebreaking centre in the Second World War. While at Bletchley Park, he led the development of the Bombe, an electromechanical device that could speed up the cracking of the German Enigma machines. The Enigma was a device used by the German forces to encode messages (see Figure 6.3). Encryption was achieved through a complex system made up of the plugboard and rotors, giving a staggering 158 million, million, million possible settings. What's more, the settings were changed daily.

In cracking the Enigma, Turing and his team recognised and exploited a crucial weakness in that no letter was ever represented as itself in an encrypted message. Knowing this, and using 'cribs', which were small sections of known decryptions, the Bombe machine (see Figure 6.4) they designed and built could automate a mathematical process of deduction to whittle down the staggering number of possible Enigma combinations to a far more manageable amount for cracking. After his work on the Bombe, Turing turned his intellectual curiosity to the even more complex German Naval Enigma

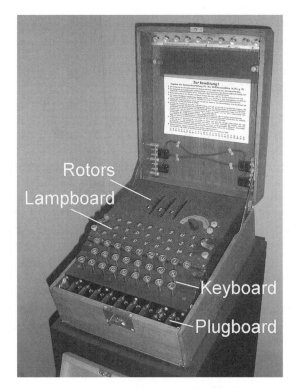

Figure 6.3   A German Enigma machine

Figure 6.4   A working replica of the Bombe at Bletchley Park Museum

system, which others thought unbreakable. Again, it was via his ingenious application of mathematical logic that he was able to conceive a process of conquering these too. Many historians believe Turing's work shortened the length of the war by around two years.

STEM link to mathematics

Along with his work breaking the Enigma codes, Turing pioneered the development of the modern-day computer. In 1936 he published the idea of a 'universal computing machine': the theory that it should be possible to create a machine to solve any possible mathematical problem for which an algorithm could be written. It was this theoretical contribution by Turing that drove the development of early computers, including those developed at the University of Manchester, including the 'Baby' and the 'Manchester Mark 1'. Indicative of his ahead-of-the-times thinking, while these early machines were being constructed, Turing had already turned his thinking to artificial intelligence (though this phrase had yet to be coined). Pondering the question: 'Can machines think?' Turing published a paper in 1950 which set out to answer this question. He devised a test known as the 'Turing Test', which remains today as a benchmark in the development of artificial intelligence.

Reflective activity

Do your learners think computers could one day be intelligent? Could they pose questions about this?

- *Could a computer write a poem?*
- *Could a computer talk to you?*
- *Can computers think and share their thoughts?*
- *Can a computer play chess? Does this mean they are intelligent?*
- *Can a computer think of something original?*

Turing was a visionary thinker with near unrivalled academic intellect fuelling his curiosity. His work breaking the Enigma codes undoubtedly saved thousands of lives in the Second World War. When reading about all Turing achieved in the relatively short life he had, it is hard not to be curious about what other ground-breaking contributions he might have gone on to make in the field of computer science and mathematics should he have lived out the entirety of his life.

Why is curiosity important in computing?

Some might think computers destroy creativity and reduce curiosity, but it can be argued that indeed the opposite is true. Computers and the Internet enable curious minds, and our greatest thinkers and entrepreneurs now use computers, and the connectivity the Internet brings, as a basis for the most innovative ideas: phone and tablet apps, social media platforms and projects funded through crowdfunding sites, for example.

It is hard to think of something which has changed the world more in recent times than the invention of the World Wide Web (WWW), but had it not been for the curiosity of a pioneering British computer scientist, Tim Berners-Lee, this life-changing invention may have never have come into existence. To explain how Berners-Lee created the WWW, we must first take a step back and look at the creation of the Internet.

The Internet is an infrastructure of computers and other devices connected across the planet: it is hardware. A large portion of the Internet is made up of cables spanning the beds of the world's oceans. If you're curious to learn more about this vast network of cables, visit: www.submarinecablemap.com. The Internet began its life in the 1960s when computers at several U.S. institutions were connected to exchange data – at the time it was called the ARPANET. Over the following years it grew in size as more computers in the USA and then across the globe were connected. However, in its early days, the connected computers spoke different languages, and so it took a computer scientist considerable effort to transfer anything across it. This was soon to change.

In 1980 Berners-Lee was working as a programmer at CERN. While at CERN, he was frustrated with the process of exchanging information between computers speaking different languages. He ended up writing several programs to convert data from one system to another. Then he became curious about the wider scope of this problem. Berners-Lee explains on his web page for children, which describe his achievements, that he started thinking to himself: 'Is there a better way?' and 'Can't we fix this problem for good?' (www.w3.org/People/Berners-Lee/Kids.html). In 1984 Berners-Lee had the opportunity to explore this question, as he took a job at CERN tasked with creating a system to share the results of staff's experiments. Over the following years, Berners-Lee and his team developed the main building blocks of the WWW, including: Hypertext Markup Language (HTML), Universal Resource Locator (URL) and Hypertext Transfer Protocol (HTTP).

```
</header>
<div class="block publication-content">
  <div class="inner-block floated-children">
    <div class="govspeak">
<h3 id="purpose-of-study">Purpose of study</h3>

<p>A high-quality computing education equips pupils to use computational thinking and creativity to understand
and change the world. Computing has deep links with mathematics, science and design and technology, and provides
insights into both natural and artificial systems.  The core of computing is computer science, in which pupils
are taught the principles of information and computation, how digital systems work and how to put this knowledge
to use through programming. Building on this knowledge and understanding, pupils are equipped to use information
technology to create programs, systems and a range of content. Computing also ensures that pupils become
digitally literate — able to use, and express themselves and develop their ideas through, information and
communication technology — at a level suitable for the future workplace and as active participants in a digital
world.</p>

<h3 id="aims">Aims</h3>

<p>The national curriculum for computing aims to ensure that all pupils:</p>
```

Figure 6.5 An extract of HTML code from the DfE's National Curriculum for computing web page (www.gov.uk/government/publications/national-curriculum-in-england-computing-programmes-of-study/national-curriculum-in-england-computing-programmes-of-study#key-stage-1)

HTML is the language web pages are written in (see an extract of HTML code in Figure 6.5). Web pages are stored in web servers connected to the Internet in HTML code. When we view a web page the HTML code is transmitted across the Internet as packets of data and your web browser (Internet Explorer or Mozilla Firefox, for example) translates the code to display the page. The process by which the transfer of this data is achieved was defined by HTTP. This specifies what happens when we click any link to view a web page. In order to locate where on the Internet web pages might be stored, we need a location system, and that is where the URL system comes in. An example of a URL is www. manchester.ac.uk.

Since Berners-Lee's pioneering work at CERN in the late 1980s, the Internet and WWW have grown exponentially. It is estimated that over 4.9 billion devices are now connected to the Internet ('Gartner says 4.9 Billion', 2014) with the WWW topping 1 billion web sites (twitter.com/timberners_lee/status/511988109211627520). It has undoubtedly changed the way we live our lives, as we now shop online; bank online, watch films online, and even meet our future spouses online.

It may be argued that WWW is also now the greatest hotbed for curiosity. As it has grown, those creating the content of the web have become more diverse. While in the early days it was predominantly businesses and organisations, more and more individuals and small groups now create online content. Blogs, vlogs and podcasts about people's hobbies and experiences make up a large portion of the WWW, as do forums where groups can discuss common interests; such websites provide the opportunity for people to share what makes them curious, satisfy curiosities they may have and read about the curiosities of others.

The WWW has also led to mass collaboration. Perhaps the greatest example being that of Wikipedia, a free online encyclo-paedia with close to 5 million articles. Wikipedia's content has been written entirely by the online community which it serves and its development has been driven by those who are curious about knowledge and the spirit of enquiry.

 Reflective activity

Could your class create a wiki or blog? What would it look like? Who would contribute to:

- *a topic-based wiki/blog?*
- *a year group wiki/blog?*
- *a sport-based wiki/blog?*
- *a diary-style wiki/blog?*

Why not sign up to the Quadblogging website (http://quad blogging.com) where your blog can be matched with three other blogs to give your learners a genuine audience for their writing, and be curious about what others are blogging.

Curiosity not only aided the invention of the WWW, but also the remarkable services which have evolved in the online world. Back in the mid-1990s, two doctoral students at Stanford University, Larry Page and Sergy Brin, were curious whether they could develop a better system for searching the WWW. Their curiosity drove them to develop a ranking system for web pages returned through a search and, as reported by Smale (2004), after securing around a $1 million investment they launched their search engine, Google, on 7 September 1998. Initially, Google received around 10,000 queries a day. Today that figure is around3.5 billion (that's around 40,000 per second) and Google is worth around $360 billion.

 Reflective activity

If you are curious about what this staggering volume of searches looks like, then visit: www.internetlivestats.com/one-second/ #google-band

When Harvard student Mark Zuckerberg started TheFace Book in 2003, it was to connect students at his university. Zuckerberg was curious about the benefits of having a central network of contacts for everyone that worked and studied at Harvard. He was also frustrated Harvard hadn't created it already: 'It was the kind of silly thing it would take Harvard a couple of years to get around to', he said in an interview in 2004 (Tabak, 2004). Zuckerberg decided to act on his curiosity and create TheFacebook. Since then, TheFacebook has become simply Facebook, and has grown to be the world's largest social media site with 1,490 million users and a company valuation of around $250 billion (Monica, 2015). And what has fuelled this phenomenal growth? Why are 91 per cent of American millennials (15–34-year-olds) users of Facebook? What drives 65 per cent of all Facebook users to check the site every single day, scanning through their news feeds to see what they might find or miss ('How millennials use', 2015)? Surely it is curiosity itself.

Curiosity underpinned Tim Berners-Lee and his team's work in creating the WWW. Once in existence, the WWW has become an arena itself to be shaped by curiosity, including the curiosity of individuals who have gone on to own the fastest growing companies of all time. It is not a coincidence that many of these companies serve curiosity in its different forms. Whether it be researching through Google, or observing the lives of others through social media, a common theme here is connectivity. When asked if the WWW had made us more intelligent, Berners-Lee said 'No, it has made us more connected'. It is this connectivity, this instant on-tap access to information which, if used in the right way, can invigorate our curiosity in the twenty-first century.

> ### ⊞ Reflective activity
>
> *Are you curious about computing pioneers? Along with Turing and Berners-Lee, there have been many others who have pioneered the world of computing. Do you know who the computing pioneers are in Figure 6.6? Are you curious to find out what they accomplished? Turn to the end of this chapter to find out more.*

Figure 6.6   Three computing pioneers

Skills in computing that are linked to/draw out curiosity

Computing presents a wealth of opportunities to both draw upon, and develop, learners' curiosity. At the heart of the shift from ICT to computing is the idea of empowering learners with the skills to create with technology; it is through developing these skills that we enable a new creative outlet for learners' curiosity in the digital world. It is also by developing their understanding of the technology in the world around them that we fuel their curiosity. As Loewenstein (1994) argued, it is hard to be curious about something we know nothing about.

Learning the skills to program is a cornerstone of computing. Programming may be thought of as a two-step process in which we first employ computational thinking to analyse a problem and generate some form of design for a solution, and then code this solution in a programming language. As learners develop their programming skills, their curiosity leads them to realise the power of programming as a creative tool. At first it is learners' curiosity which drives them to explore the function of various codes in a programming language. As learners' competence in coding then increases, their curiosity shifts focus to contexts and problems they can solve by coding. To fully embrace their curiosity, learners should be given the opportunity to develop their programming skills through creative programming projects inspired by their topics and interests. This is discussed further in Chapter 7. As well as learning to code programs with on-screen outputs, learners of all age ranges should have the opportunity to create programs on, or that interact with, hardware, such as the Codebug© shown in Figure 6.7. Hardware adds an extra dimension to computing, making things move, such as dancing floor robots, or reacting, such as a burglar alarm. These inputs and outputs in the real world reveal to learners the power of programming. It also feeds their curiosity about what they could make using the hardware and how they could make it. A case study in Chapter 7 explores in more detail a range of appropriate computing hardware for Key Stages 1 and 2.

Learning how to make things is only one half of the story when programming; learning how to make things better is the other half. When writing programs it is not unusual for them to have errors, known as bugs. The process of finding and fixing these bugs is called debugging. It is not unusual for 50 per cent of time in the development of commercial software to be spent on testing and debugging. Loewenstein (1994) said our curiosity is induced when we become aware of a gap in our understanding, and Piaget (1969) suggested curiosity appears when our expectations are violated; bugs fulfil both these conditions: not only is the program not doing as we expect, but since computers are entirely deterministic machines, the bug must be a result of the learner's programming – a gap in their understanding perhaps? Curiosity underpins the debugging process. If we are not curious as to why

Figure 6.7   A Codebug© (www.codebug.org.uk)

something is not working, it is unlikely we will be motivated to fix it.

There are often different ways to code a program which give the same output. One, however, might be unnecessarily complex, while the other might be neat, concise and created in a way which can be reused in the future to save time. At Key Stage 3 learners explore functions and procedures, where sections of regularly used code are packaged up and drawn upon within the main program when required, to prevent unnecessary duplication. Developing programming skills such as these requires an appreciation of what it means to be an efficient coder and this too is driven by curiosity: Could we have coded this differently? How? What benefits would a different approach bring? Could we have written more efficient code? How? Could we have written code in a way in which we can use it elsewhere in our program? Or again in the future?

As an example, both sets of code in Figure 6.8 will draw an octagon. However, the right-hand solution is clearly quicker to write and can also draw an octagon of any size by changing just one size value. What's more, by simply changing the turn angle and the number of times the steps are repeated, this section of code can be used to draw any other regular polygon.

STEM link
to
mathematics

 Reflective activity

What would the values for a triangle or pentagon be? And for a decagon? Can this bit of code be used to draw a circle?

An important theme in the preceding paragraph is the relationship between curiosity and evaluation. Evaluation is about making systematic and objective judgements. Such judgements are made through asking questions, and it is here that curiosity plays its part. Without being curious as to whether a program is working, or whether we've coded an efficient solution, learners aren't motivated to ask these questions and advance their learning.

As you read the preceding section on Tim Berners-Lee's invention of the WWW, you may have felt your curiosity aroused. Maybe before reading this you weren't aware that the Internet and WWW were different? Perhaps having this gap in your knowledge highlighted an aspect of interest? You began wondering what exactly these two terms meant? Maybe you started reflecting more widely on your understanding of the technology of 'going online'? Perhaps you started wondering what else you don't know about the Internet and WWW? Developing this understanding of computer networks, including the Internet, and the services they can provide, makes up part of the computing curriculum at Key Stage 2 (see Figure 6.1) and provides ample opportunities to spark and fuel learners' curiosity. Show learners the source code of a web page in HTML, for example, and we can ignite their curiosity around the notion of there being a 'language of the web'. 'What does all this text mean, what does it do and how do we learn to write it?' they might ask. In the following chapter a case study of short activities to spark and fuel learners' curiosity about computer networks is presented.

We are all aware of the saying 'curiosity killed the cat', and equally aware that curiosity was to blame for Pandora releasing evil spirits on opening her box. In both cases, the message here is that curiosity can sometimes lead us to do things against our better judgement. This type of curiosity seems to resonate with Freud's theories, as described by Aronoff (1962), of an innate

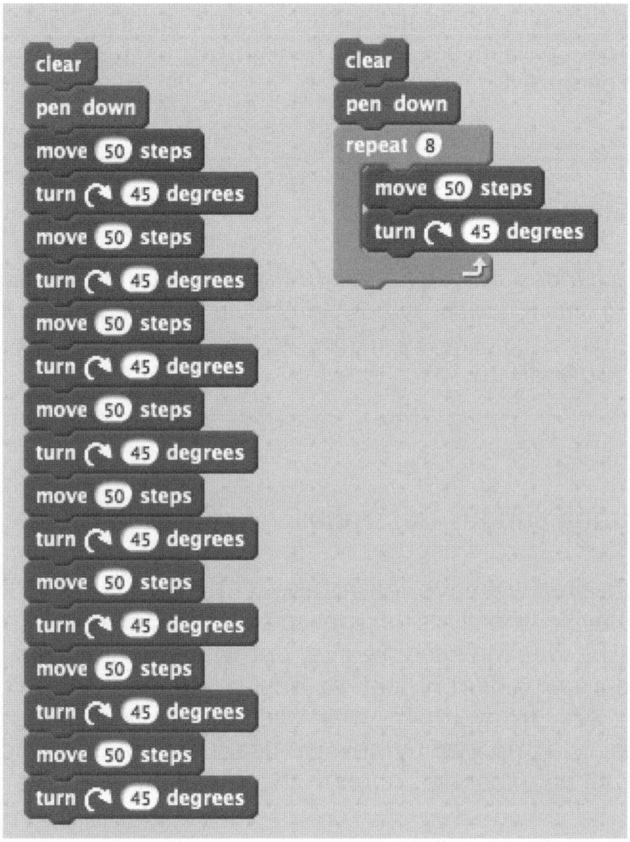

```
clear

pen down

move (50) steps

turn (45) degrees

move (50) steps

turn (45) degrees

move (50) steps

turn (45) degrees

move (50) steps

turn (45) degrees

move (50) steps

turn (45) degrees

move (50) steps

turn (45) degrees

move (50) steps

turn (45) degrees

move (50) steps

turn (45) degrees


clear

pen down

repeat (8)

    move (50) steps

    turn (45) degrees
```

Figure 6.8 Two sets of code, each of which will draw an octagon

drive coming from within, causing a desire to explore, sometimes with unintended consequences. Since this side of human curiosity undoubtedly exists, there are obvious implications for learners' E-Safety, as their curiosity leads them to explore the online world. It feels natural to be curious about those we meet, and this extends to those we meet online. However, learners should be educated about the risks of when this curiosity overrides sensible decisions around the sharing of personal information, which applies equally in both the online and offline world. Likewise, learners' curiosity could take them to inappropriate web sites and they need to know what to do if this occurs and who to tell if they have seen something they feel uncomfortable with. Finally, curiosity is often used as a tool in online fraud. Many phishing emails rely on creating a sense of curiosity in those they target, by promising money, for example. Developing learners' discernment can act as an antidote to impulsive behaviour driven by their curiosity.

For a wealth of excellent resources to support E-Safety within your school, please see: http://swgfl.org.uk/products-services/esafety/resources

---

 Reflective activity

Are you curious about what might happen if you replied to a phishing email? So was James Veitch. See his entertaining TED Talk at: www.ted.com/talks/james_veitch_this_is_what_happens_when_you_reply_to_spam_email

---

A computing curious classroom

In this chapter we have learnt about the part that curiosity has had to play in the lives of the computing pioneers which have changed the way in which we live, but what changes can we make to our learning environment to ensure our learners' computing curiosity will prosper? In this section we will discuss which resources, and importantly how we use them, can enhance curiosity. This will be expanded upon in the case studies in the following chapter.

There are a variety of programming languages available to primary schools, although some are better suited to embracing learners' curiosity than others. Scratch© is a free educational programming language developed by the Massachusetts Institute of Technology (MIT). It is a visual language, meaning programs are constructed from command blocks dragged together in the script area (Figure 6.9). The development of Scratch© was led by Mitch Resnick of MIT. Resnick and his team wanted to create a programming language in which learners could snap together blocks to build programs as easily as they could build with Lego©. He and his team succeeded, and it is the quick, intuitive, creative nature of Scratch© which makes it ideal for curious learners, as they can easily code and test the ideas their curiosity dreams up.

Kodu© is free programming language developed by Microsoft which shares the visual approach to programming. The 3D world in which Kodu© (Figure 6.10) programs are created is visually engaging for learners, and acts as a hook for their curiosity about what they could think up and create.

STEM link to mathematics

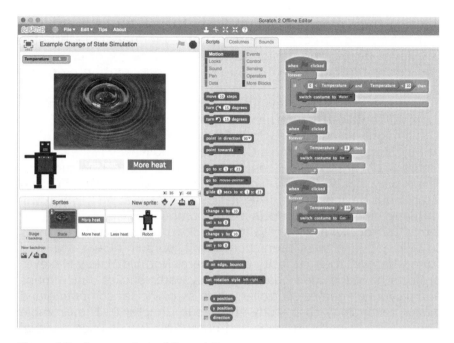

Figure 6.9   A screenshot of Scratch©

Figure 6.10   A screenshot of a game created in Kodu©. (The code for the game is not visible.)

ScratchJr© (Figure 6.11) is an app which is suited to programming at Key Stage 1. Along with ScratchJr©, apps such as Lightbot© and Daisy the Dinosaur© allow learners to develop their programming skills as they exercise their curiosity about how to code in these simple languages. Lightbot© is a level-based app designed to create a sense of challenge and curiosity about how to code the correct solution by those playing it.

As mentioned in the previous section, a computing curious classroom will contain a range of hardware for learners to use. At Key Stage 1 this might include Bee-Bots©, Roamers© or other floor turtles. At Key Stage 2, the Crumble Controller© and Makey Makey© (see Figure 6.12) are excellent resources to foster computing curiosity. The Makey Makey© (www.youtube.com/watch?v=rfQqh7iCcOU) is an input device, again designed by the team at MIT, which will turn anything which conducts a small amount of electrical current into a button. Like Scratch© it is quick to use, allowing learners to be creative in their interaction with it, pursuing ideas spawned from wherever their curiosity takes them. Notable Makey Makey© projects have included banana pianos, water bucket dance maps and playdough games controllers. A cross-curricular computing and design technology case study appears in Chapter 9. The Crumble Controller© is both an input and output device. It uses a visual

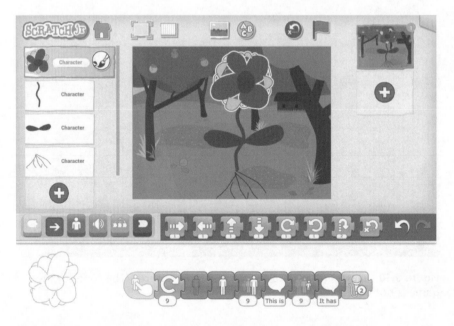

Figure 6.11 A screenshot of Scratch Junior© coding an interactive scene of the parts of a plant.

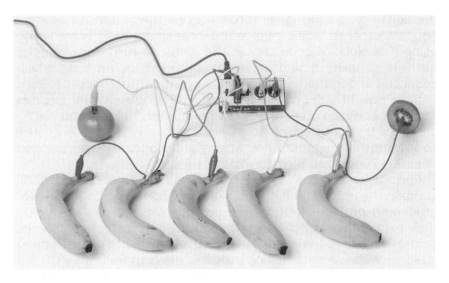

Figure 6.12   A Makey Makey© being used to create a banana keyboard (www.makeymakey.com) Joylabz LLC

programming language closely resembling Scratch© and can be used to drive motors, light lights and buzz buzzers. It opens up a world of physical computing projects with links to design technology, such as the dancing robot case study described in the next chapter. Further information on computing resources appears in the following chapter.

Just as important as the resources available to learners is the learning culture and environment in which they are used. So what ways of teaching, what pedagogies, can we use to promote curiosity in computing?

STEM link to design and technology

In the case studies in Chapter 7 the term 'tinkering' is often mentioned, as it is in the design and technology chapters of this book. There is some variety in different groups' definitions of 'tinkering'. Here we see tinkering as a 'playful, experimental, interactive style of engagement' in line with Resnick (2013). We can think of tinkering as being in opposition to a constrained linear sequence of plan, make, evaluate in which we would complete each stage before moving on to the next. When tinkering we move more freely between stages, flitting back and forth between design and make as our ideas evolve. Evaluation and refinement is happening all the time. When tinkering, learners are not entirely constrained by their original design, but are afforded the agility to pursue ideas thrown up by their curiosity as they go. This process might involve a degree of serendipity, realising using this block of code causes the motor to turn, for example, but it is curiosity acting upon the serendipitous moment which advances understanding: 'Perhaps I could get that motor to turn too and now I think I can build a car'. The curious learner exploits the links between computing, design and technology, and mathematics. It is interesting to note Seymour Papert (1993), the co-inventor of the programming language Logo, also championed tinkering (using the term 'bricolage').

Curiosity and creativity are closely related. To foster learners' curiosity in programming, we need to undertake creative programming projects with sufficient scope for learners to pursue their own ideas. To achieve this requires a degree of confidence by the teacher so that they can effectively facilitate programming lessons, with learners having scope to develop their own unique ideas. To help in this endeavour, a curious computing classroom would make good use of all funds of knowledge available, including other learners. Each school is likely to have learners whose own curiosity has led them to use languages such as Scratch© and Kodu© outside of school. Using their knowledge to support within the classroom environment is a great way of getting them to share this curiosity and enthusiasm for computing with others, and develop their own understanding further as they take on the role of teacher.

Modelling curiosity is an essential role of the teacher in a computing curious classroom. Curiosity often arises in the form of questions. These might be questions about what we want to create and how we might go about it: I wonder if I could program a drone to trace out a cube? I wonder how I could create a times table game in Scratch©? Wouldn't it be great if I could program four Bee-Bots© to dance? How could I use this piece of code? How could I improve what I have created? Thinking aloud questions like this helps both model 'being curious', and convey an enthusiasm for learning; indeed, we might say a love of learning is the main trait of a curious mind. Questions might also arise when things don't work the way they should do and we have to debug: Why isn't it...? I wonder if the bug is in...? How can I work out where the bug is? How can we make it...? What code could I use instead? It is important to model the importance of being systematically curious to work our way through errors, and reward learners' curiosity and persistence in debugging. This is explored in a case study in more detail in the following chapter.

Conclusion

This chapter has illustrated the close links between curiosity and computing. To start, it spent some time getting curious about the computing curriculum. It looked at how computing breaks down into three strands and the role of computational thinking in computing and the influence curiosity has had over the world in which we live. We might be without the web, or even without computers, had it not been for the curious minds of Tim Berners-Lee and Alan Turing. The second half of this chapter looked in more detail at the links between curiosity and specific computing skills and how we might create a computing curious classroom. These ideas will be expanded still further in the following chapter as we explore case studies on how we can enhance curiosity in primary computing.

Chapter summary

Having read this chapter you will:

- have a better developed understanding of computer science in primary education;
- appreciate the importance of curiosity in computing;
- have a better understanding of how the skills in computing enhance and utilise curiosity;
- be able to identify features of a computing curious classroom.

Curious about computing pioneers in Figure 6.6?
From left to right:

Margaret Hamilton was Director of the Software Engineering Division of the MIT Instrumentation Laboratory, which developed on-board flight software for the Apollo space program. In the picture she is standing next to a printout of the code that she and her team wrote for the Apollo 11 guidance computer, which made the moon landing possible.

Ada Lovelace was a British mathematician and writer born in 1815. She is credited with writing the first algorithm, which appears in her notes on using Charles Babbage's early mechanical general-purpose computer, the Analytical Engine. As such, Ada Lovelace is considered to be the first computer programmer.

Grace Hopper was an American computer scientist and United States Navy Rear Admiral. She was one of the first programmers of the Harvard Mark 1 computer in 1944. Hopper championed the development of machine-independent programming languages, as are used today, and popularised the term 'debugging'.

CHAPTER 7

WAYS TO ENHANCE CURIOSITY IN PRIMARY COMPUTING

Chapter objectives

After reading this chapter you will:

- have an understanding of a selection of resources suited to enhancing curiosity in computing in primary schools;
- have an understanding of what aspects of computing lessons enhance learners' curiosity;
- have an understanding of how to design computing lessons to enhance learners' curiosity.

Overview

Chapter 6 discussed the curriculum change from ICT to computing and explored how the curious minds of computing pioneers, such as Alan Turing, Tim Berners-Lee and others, had driven the invention of revolutionary technologies.

Primary STEM subjects offer a vast array of opportunities for curiosity; as part of this, computing is a subject which both depends upon, but which can also enhance curiosity. The discussion in Chapter 6 illustrated the importance of curiosity in developing an understanding of how to program, as well as persevering through the process of debugging. As learners enhance their computing skills, they will develop a new medium in which to exercise their curiosity, as they learn to be creative programmers.

In this chapter we will provide case studies which exemplify the themes discussed in Chapter 6. Throughout the case studies, signature characteristics which draw out curiosity will be discussed. The chapter will show that a common theme is the 'open' nature of activities, allowing learners to be creative as their curiosity leads their work. The case studies have links with other subjects, both STEM subjects and beyond. For example, the robot dance-off project links to design and technology, mathematics and science; and the network activities link to geography. It will also explore the relationship between computational thinking and curiosity in the context of science enquiries.

The case studies answer the following questions: What is the activity? Where is the curiosity? What do I need? In answering these questions, an overview of the activity is given along with a description on how it fits with curiosity and how to conduct the activity with your learners.

Promoting curiosity in primary computing

There are several key elements which need to be in place to promote curiosity in computing. First, the context of learners' projects needs to appeal to their interests, and/or make links to wider topics, to help hook learners into the tasks. Ensuring learners see real-world applications of the skills they are developing is vital since it encourages them to be curious about what they could go on to create in the future, as their skills develop further. Building learners' confidence in computing is important, as in all subjects, as discussed earlier through Dweck's (2006) work on growth mindset. As learners achieve tasks and build confidence in themselves as programmers, they'll be more excited and willing to take on new challenges thrown up by their curiosity.

A key theme throughout this book is the importance of questioning. Questions are an expression of curiosity, and so modelling and encouraging questioning is essential to fostering curious minds. This could be questions about blocks of code, or wonderings about what we might want to create and how we go about it. As discussed in Chapter 6, questioning is particularly important when debugging. It is also important that learners see bugs and debugging as an expected part of their programming journey. A learning culture which rewards perseverance in working through these bugs will produce learners not only capable of generating ideas for programs but also equipped with the perseverance to see them through to creation. Part of debugging is also knowing where to go for help. Model to learners where we can find information to help us, such as in online videos, searching online, blog posts or by asking those around us such as pupils and staff.

Promoting curiosity in computing is …?

This section considers pedagogical approaches that can help to cultivate and maintain levels of curiosity in computing.

Curiosity in computing is … providing a rich environment

In offering his ideas on how we might teach computing, Miles Berry (2013b) looked to the work of German educationalist Friedrich Fröbel who conceptualised a form of Early Years education he termed the kindergarten. Berry (2013b) explored several aspects of Fröbel's vision for education, including his gardens and gifts. Fröbel's kindergarten gardens were unique in their richness as an environment for learners to explore (indeed, letting their curiosity lead them), and his 'gifts' were a set of progressive educational toys, such as building blocks of increasing complexity. Berry (2013b) highlights the importance of offering learners an equally rich garden of devices and software for computing, and points out the similarities with the building block approach to programming in MIT's Scratch© to that of Fröbel's gifts; indeed, he explains it is not merely coincidence that Scratch© was developed in MIT's lifelong kindergarten group (https://llk.media.mit.edu).

So what might we consider a rich environment of software and hardware in primary schools for teaching computer science? And how might factors such as cost and hardware devices (laptops, tablets, PC or Mac) influence our choice? To answer these questions, and help you prepare a rich computing environment at your school, the first case study reviews the equipment used in an English primary school.

CASE STUDY

Resources used in one English primary school

Curriculum links: Mathematics, Design and Technology

The two tables below (Tables 7.1 and 7.2) detail a selection of the resources used to teach computer science in Key Stages 1 and 2 in one

(Continued)

(Continued)

primary school. Within the tables a 'Curiosity Capacity' field describes how the resources work well with learners' curious minds.

Key Stage 1

Table 7.1   Resources used for Key Stage 1

Resource	Description	Curiosity Capacity
Bee-Bot© www.tts-group.co.uk/ shops/tts/Products/ PD1723538/Bee-Bot-Floor-Robot/	The Bee-Bot© is a programmable floor turtle suitable for EYFS and Key Stage 1. The Bee-Bot's© interface is easy to use consisting of five commands.	Since the Bee-Bot© is easy to use, giving learners time to play with and explore it allows them to exercise their curiosity while developing their understanding of the commands and how a program is created.
ScratchJr© www.scratchjr.org	ScratchJr© is a free app available on Android and iOS. It is essentially a Key Stage 1 version of Scratch©, being developed by members of the same team at MIT.	ScratchJr© can be used creatively with learners' curious minds dreaming up, designing and coding their own animations, interactive scenes or simple games.

Key Stage 2

Table 7.2   Resources used for Key Stage 2

Resource	Description	Curiosity capacity
Scratch https://scratch.mit.edu	Scratch© is a free programming language for PC or Mac. There is an online version of Scratch© 2 and a community to share your programs.	Scratch© was 'designed with tinkering in mind' (Resnick, 2013). Learners can quickly and easily explore what commands do and what they can code. The online Scratch© community fuels curiosity

STEM link to mathematics

STEM link to mathematics

STEM link to mathematics

Resource	Description	Curiosity capacity	
		by sharing what others have created. These projects can be 'remixed', whereby learners can delve into, and edit, the code of others' programs.	
Kodu© www.kodugamelab. com	Kodu© is a programming language from Microsoft available free on PC (also available at a small cost on XBox). It is particularly suited to creating games.	Kodu© is intuitive to use. Learners can quickly create 3D games with graphics comparable with those available to purchase. Seeing great results achieved quickly fuels learners' curiosity about what they could go on to create.	STEM link to mathematics
Lego Education WeDo© education.lego.com/ en-gb/lesi/elementary/ lego-education-wedo	Lego Education WeDo© sets include sensors (tilt and motion) and a motor. These are connected to Mac or PC via the hub. These devices can be used with either Scratch© or the Lego Education WeDo© programming language.	The Lego Education WeDo© resources use a construction technique learners are likely to be familiar with. This makes it quick for learners to prototype their ideas. Given the resource interfaces with Scratch, learners can draw on their understanding of this language to quickly try out their ideas.	STEM link to design and technology
Makey Makey© www.makeymakey. com Joylabz LLC	The Makey Makey© was developed by two students at the MIT Media Lab (under the supervision of Scratch's© creator Mitch Resnick). It is billed as 'an invention kit for	The inventors of the Makey Makey© believe everyone is 'creative, inventive and imaginative', almost certainly symptoms of a curious mind. They invented the Makey Makey© to help us express this.	STEM link to design and technology

(Continued)

(Continued)

Resource	Description	Curiosity capacity
	anyone' and allows the user to turn everyday items into inputs for a computer.	
Crumble Controller© redfernelectronics. co.uk/crumble/ CrumbleBot© 4tronix.co.uk/store/ index.php?rt= product/ product&product_ id=493 4Tronix	The Crumble Controller© is an easy-to-use programmable controller which can drive two motors, LEDs and take inputs from switches and various sensors. It is programmed in a visual language very similar to Scratch. The CrumbleBot© provides a chassis for a Crumble Controller© to be attached to create a simple robot.	The makers of the Crumble© and CrumbleBot© explain that their products are 'designed for tinkering'. Crocodile clips quickly connect different components allowing learners to easily test and explore their ideas. As the programming language is visual, and similar to Scratch, it too is easier for learners to quickly code programs.
RaspberryPi© www.raspberrypi. org	The RapsberryPi© is a small affordable computer developed in part to help the learning of computer science.	The diverse range of ways in which the RaspberryPi© has been used by schools and hobbyists around the world is testament to its ability to indulge the curious mind. One example is the use of the Pi as a tracker in high-altitude ballooning https:// opensource.com/life/15/9/ pi-sky-high-altitude-ballooning-raspberry-pi

STEM link to design and technology

STEM link to mathematics

STEM link to design and technology

STEM link to mathematics

This case study has presented examples of the range of software and hardware used to engage the curious minds of learners in computer science. Of course there are many alternative resources available, and new products are coming on to the market all the time. To help ensure your school provides learners with a rich curiosity friendly environment, take a moment to consider the questions in the reflective activity below about the resources you have or intend to purchase.

 Reflective activity

The questions below will help you reflect on the resources you have in your school and if/how they work with learners' curiosity.

- *List the resources you have for Key Stages 1 and 2. Do you have a range for both key stages? Or at least some resources?*
- *Do the programming languages you are using allow for learners to be creative? Are they easy to explore and tinker with? Are they low-entry high-ceiling tools?*
- *Are you providing learners with experience of physical computing in both Key Stage 1 (floor turtles) and Key Stage 2 (control equipment)?*

The cost of equipment can pose a barrier when resourcing schools, so it is worth contacting local high schools and university computer science departments as many run equipment libraries which loan equipment to schools, e.g. The University of Manchester Computer Science Department www.cs.manchester.ac.uk/schools-and-colleges/raspberry-pi/.

Curiosity in computing is … about creative projects

Equally as important as considering what resources will make up our rich environment, is considering how we plan for learners to engage with them. The potential of rich programming languages, such as Scratch©, to foster learners' curiosity will be diminished if it is used in an overly prescriptive manner leaving little or no room for learners' curiosity to drive their creativity. Indeed, returning to Fröbel, his impetus for the time spent creating rich gardens was an appreciation of the importance of letting learners play in them and take part in creative activities.

Let's explore

We can translate Fröbel's emphasis on child-led play to our context by affording learners time to explore resources we have gathered for them; stepping back as a teacher and letting learners' curiosity drive their learning. Play and exploration is an approach used more often in Early Years and Foundation Stage and Key Stage 1, but it can be equally valuable when working with older learners. This can work particularly well when introducing a new programming language or piece of hardware, in which learners quickly find themselves becoming aware of what they don't know and thus, according to Loewenstein (1994), have their curiosity aroused. Pairing learners, or getting them to work in small groups, using regular mini plenaries to share their discoveries as they explore illustrates how curiosity can drive forward learning. This 'social constructivist' (Vygotsky, 1978) approach can better enable both a group's and individual's curiosity.

It is worth noting here that a completely unguided approach might not suit all learners, and some guided discovery may help subsequent pupil-led exploration. Indeed, Loewenstein (1994) argued that we cannot be curious about something we know nothing about, and so we might consider this guided discovery acting as a curiosity 'activation energy', moving learners from not knowing what they don't know to knowing what they don't know, and so fuelling their desire to find out. Following a period of exploration, we can then plan projects which still afford room for curiosity to drive learning, and the key to achieving this is through creative open projects, such as the examples given in the following case studies.

CASE STUDY

Robot dance-off

This activity was mentioned briefly in Chapter 1. Learners work in groups to design and construct a robot which they program to dance to music. The robots compete in a robot 'dance-off' which is judged to determine a winning team.

A great stimulus for this activity is to watch a video of the Hexapod Championships www.youtube.com/watch?v=pXMnbNoccgA

Figure 7.1 shows an example of a robot. Robots were constructed from card paper and wood wheels and axe. Two separate motors power the two front wheels. There is a multicoloured LED in each arm. The motors and LEDs are controlled by a Crumble Controller© mounted in the body. The first stages of this activity are primarily design and technology focused, as learners design and make their robots. As discussed in Chapter 8, a design and technology project requires a clear design brief. Here the brief is to create a robot for the purpose of dancing for the audience of judges. This leads to functional and creative requirements, as the robot needs to both incorporate the electronics hardware and look great dancing! The control hardware used in the robot is the Crumble Controller©. This is used to drive a motor on each back wheel and flash the robot's LED eyes.

STEM link to design and technology

Figure 7.1   Dancing robots

Once groups have constructed their robot, they program its dance routine. This is a creative task as learners invent dance moves and a dance routine to appropriate music: 'Let's get it to spin as that cymbal crashes' or 'It needs to wait there until the next part starts'. This project might even include learners composing their own music in which further National Curriculum computing

(Continued)

(Continued)

STEM link
to
mathematics

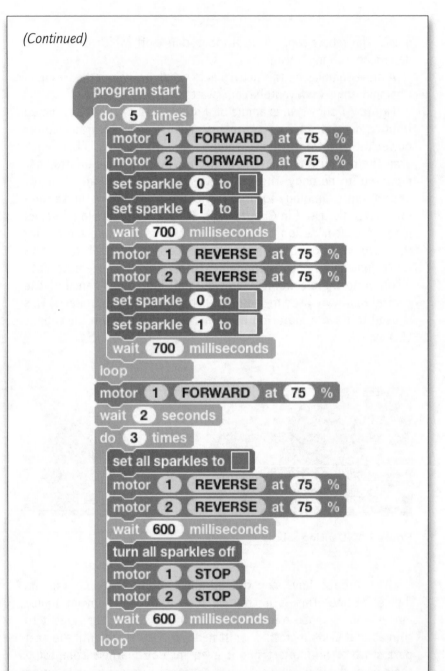

Figure 7.2   An example of a section of code used to make a robot start dancing

and music objectives can be covered. The task of designing the dance draws upon a wide range of computational thinking skills: learners will decompose the dance routine into sections, for example, as well as write the algorithms for each section and identify patterns during the routine. Learners then code their routines in a programming language to bring their robots to life '(see Figure 7.2 for an example of a section of code used to make the robot dance using the two motors and getting the LEDs to flash). Once all groups have written the code for their robots, a 'dance-off' can be arranged and a winner decided. Points can be awarded for construction, complexity in coding and creative flare in the creation of a dazzling dance display.

As mentioned at the start of this section, the creative open nature of the challenge makes this activity ideal for engaging the curious minds of learners. Throughout the activity, learners are able to exercise their curiosity, first in the design and creation of their robot, and second in the creation of its dance routine. However, to really place curiosity at the heart of this activity, we must take a moment to discuss the iterative nature of designing and making in this project. In this activity learners create a design for both their robot and for its dance routine, and at this stage are free to exercise their curiosity. Could we make the body from...? I wonder if this material would be suitable? Could we get it to move forward while spinning? This design stage is full of wonder about what they could create. As learners move on to make the robot, we must continue to give curiosity room to lead – for example they might discover a novel way of joining materials which gives rise to new ideas for their robot's construction. Likewise, when programming the dance routine, it is difficult for learners to entirely understand what is and isn't possible at the design stage, and the stimulus of having their robot moving in front of them will certainly spawn new ideas. This is why adopting an agile approach to the project is important, since if we are to nurture learners' curiosity we must encourage them to pursue these ideas and not entirely constrain them to what they had initially 'planned' to do. We should encourage learners to alter designs as they go while still bearing the original design brief in mind. This agile iterative approach to design and make characterised by learners flitting between ideas (head) and doing (hand) is explained further in Chapter 8.

> STEM link to design and technology

CASE STUDY

Interactive scenes in ScratchJr©

This case study illustrates a creative programming activity aimed at Key Stage 1 (Year 2). The stimulus for this project was nocturnal animals and learners were challenged to create an interactive scene.

Learners first spent time exploring ScratchJr©. In doing so they started to discover what the language enabled them to do, for example getting sprites (programmable objects) to move, or to say things. They then designed their program, which included sketching the animals which would feature in their program and writing the algorithm detailing what these animals would do, for example how they might move and what they might say. As for the robot design above, this was a creative process, giving scope for learners to pursue their own ideas. These ideas draw upon their experience from exploring the language, reiterating the importance of this stage.

Figure 7.3 shows two pupils coding their design. As discussed above, the extent to which we insist learners code exactly what they specified in their design will influence the degree to which their curiosity can still lead in the coding stage. It may be that learners discover a new command which they think they can use to make the owl fly across the night sky. We shouldn't stop them from trying this, but should ask them to reflect on their design – are there any other changes they now want to make? This also illustrates to learners how curiosity-driven exploration feeds into their learning.

STEM link
to science

Figure 7.3   Pupils coding their nocturnal scene in ScratchJr©

Curiosity in computing is ... enhanced through collaboration

Both MIT's Scratch© and Microsoft's Kodu© embrace a sense of sharing and collaboration as they have websites where programs can be published and 'remixed' by others. By setting up school accounts, learners' programs can be shared with others across the globe (Figure 7.4). This feeds learners' curiosity about how others may alter their program, or how they might alter the work of others. What changes did they make? How did they make these changes? Similarly, as learners browse programs created by other users, they may become curious about how these were coded. To satisfy this curiosity they can download the programs and explore the code. To enable learners in your school to share their programs and explore remixing the work of others, sign up for a Scratch© account at scratch.mit.edu and for Kodu© at www. kodugamelab.com

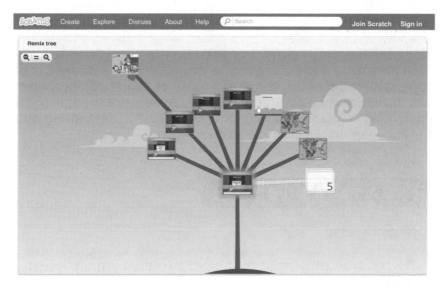

Figure 7.4   A Scratch© remix tree showing users creating remixes of a program

Curiosity in computing is ... about sparking learners' interests

Chapter 1 explored several models of curiosity, including that of Loewenstein (1994). To recap, Loewenstein (1994) suggests curiosity is aroused when we become aware of what we don't know. It follows that it is difficult to become curious about something we know nothing about, as we don't know what we don't know. As teachers, we are aware that our role is to provide experiences which develop learners' understanding; however, we might not have previously considered that in doing so what is equally important is making them aware of gaps in their understanding, and thus igniting their curiosity. This philosophy was concisely summed up by the poet, Anatole France, who said:

> *The whole art of teaching is only the art of awakening the natural curiosity of young minds for the purpose of satisfying it afterwards. (France, 1881)*

There is much opportunity in computing, as in the other subjects in this book, to move learners from a position of 'unknown unknowns' to a degree of awareness which activates their curiosity. Indeed, this mechanism may explain why giving learners time to explore new programming languages or hardware can be so valuable. Below are three examples of short activities which can introduce the Key Stage 2 computer network content of the computing National Curriculum (DfE, 2013), harnessing and fuelling learners' curiosity to find out more.

CASE STUDY

Network safari

STEM link to science

This activity aimed at Key Stage 2 learners takes them on a hunt around school to discover all the devices connected to the schools network, including the server (don't let them switch it off!), switches, wireless routers, printers and computers. They can mark these on a sketch map of the school covering Key Stage 2 geography objectives and even go off site looking for the nearest 'green cabinet', which is where local networks connect. After identifying the different devices, they can get curious about the purpose of each, identifying what it does and why it is needed.

To help spark learners' curiosity you might ask if they have ever wondered what the device with all the wires coming out of it in the corner of the library/cupboard/classroom is for (like those pictured in Figure 7.5). Have they ever wondered why they can save their work on one computer and open it on another? Or maybe they've spotted small boxes on the wall with flashing lights and wondered what they do? They might have a suspicion they allow the tablet in their hand to access web pages, or maybe let it print, or perhaps both? Sharing these ideas reveals learners' existing understanding and misconceptions. You may yourself as a teacher initially be learning with your learners.

Figure 7.5   A server and a network switch

The act of investigating what they can find in their school, by following connecting cables and hunting out wireless routers, for example, feeds an interest about how the various devices are connected and their purpose. Would we still be able to access the Internet without this? This new understanding fuels curiosity in different contexts. How is the wireless router in a home the same or different to the server and switch in school for example? Learners could create a glossary of terms describing aspects of the network, or label different devices in school with information about what they do.

STEM link
to science

CASE STUDY

Where in the world (visual traceroute)?

A key objective of the Key Stage 2 curriculum is for learners to understand the difference between the Internet and the World Wide Web as discussed in Chapter 6. This involves developing an understanding that the world wide web is made up of web pages stored on web servers (computers connected to the Internet). A great way to illustrate this is to use a web-based visual traceroute program such as http://en.dnstools.ch/visual-traceroute.html. A visual traceroute program provides an illustration of data travelling across the Internet to the web server holding the web page requested, as shown in Figure 7.6.

Learners can use visual traceroute to become more curious about where in the world web pages are stored. Where is their favourite web page stored for example? Which countries do they find store the most/least web pages? Perhaps they might wonder how many different countries they can find hosting web pages? They might then start to wonder how web pages travel across the Internet, which could lead into activities modelling the Internet or how search engines work.

Figure 7.6   Visual traceroute of location of www.google.com server

CASE STUDY

Remixing web pages (Mozilla X-Ray goggles)

HTML is the language that web pages are written in. It is HTML code which is transferred across the Internet when you view a web page, and your browser (e.g. Internet Explorer, Google Chrome) interprets this code to present the page. You can view the HTML code for any web page by following the steps for your browser detailed here: www.computer hope.com/issues/ch000746.htm. While learning HTML is not explicitly a requirement of the computing National Curriculum (DfE, 2013), tools such as Mozilla's X-Ray goggles© and Thimble© make it more than possible for learners to start to learn about HTML coding in a fun, creative way at upper Key Stage 2.

Using X-Ray goggles© learners can see and edit the HTML code behind websites. By editing the code, they can change the content of the website. See how in Figure 7.7 a reference to STEM has been added to the webpage by the author.

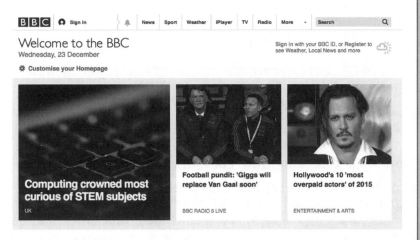

Figure 7.7   BBC webpage edited using Mozilla X-Ray goggles

Thimble©, also created by Mozilla (Figure 7.8), is an easy-to-use online tool which can be used to code and share web pages in HTML.

(Continued)

(Continued)

Its intuitive-to-use interface shows your web page as you are building it, making it ideal for experimenting with, allowing learners to exercise their curiosity about different HTML tags.

Figure 7.8 Screenshot of Mozilla Thimble©

 Reflective activity

Are you curious to learn more about HTML? Why not have a go at Codecademy's online introduction to HTML coding here: www. codecademy.com – you'll be surprised how easy it is.

Curiosity in computing ... is about dealing with bugs

Bugs happen. It is very rare for someone, be it professional pro-grammer, enthusiastic hobbyist or school-based learner, to code their program and it work just as intended, first time. That said, it is also rare for learners to wait until their program is entirely finished before they test it; their curiosity prevents them from doing so. This is not a bad thing and in fact should be encouraged, since debugging 'as you go' allows learners to more easily isolate where a bug might be. Indeed, even better is to purposely identify how you might decompose your program to code it in sections to help with debugging. The presence of bugs naturally arouses learners' curiosity. You can tell this by listening to learners' lan-guage as they are coding, when you will often hear the 'why' questions characteristic of a curious mind 'Why is/isn't it doing ...?'

'Why won't it...?' Bugs, like mistakes in other subjects, provide a valuable opportunity to advance learning and develop curiosity, if they are responded to in the correct way.

To consider how we can best respond to bugs, let's refer back to the growth mindset work of Dweck (2006). The growth mindset approach encourages us to reflect on what we attribute success to. If we attribute success to an innate fixed intelligence, we are saying to ourselves we can't get better at anything: we're either good at it or we aren't. If, however, we attribute success to our hard work, practice and persistence then this is something we can ramp up our efforts in, giving ourselves the opportunity to improve. A growth mindset approach to debugging also values curiosity; it encourages us to get stuck into the code, curious about where the bug might be and what we can do about it; curious to see if we can learn what we did wrong and what to do differently next time. Our curiosity helps us generate the questions we need answers to: Is this/that part of code correct? How do I know? I wonder if? Let's try... Do I understand how this piece of code works? Do I really? How do I know?

Building debugging power

Despite the preceding discussion, you may find learners aren't as proactive debuggers as you would like; perhaps they do not appear driven by the same power of curiosity as you would wish. They might just want you to fix their code for them. Bagge (2015) highlights the prevalence of 'learned helplessness' in computing, where learners simply want others to do it for them, be that the teacher, teaching assistant or other learners. They just don't appear to display the curiosity-driven investigative approach debugging demands. Bagge (2015) feels this has emerged partly from a culture of valuing the end product rather than the process, and the willingness of too many teachers to jump in too quickly to solve problems for their learners. Adopting a strategy of learned helplessness hoping for a quick fix is the antithesis of curiosity and should be challenged. The activities and ideas below can encourage learners to be curious about bugs in their programs and in doing so build their debugging power.

Create the right culture: Best Bugs

Create a culture in which it is okay to have bugs, make clear these are part of the programming process. Bugs can be celebrated as learning opportunities by listing them on a 'Best Bugs' board as in Figure 7.9. Celebrate those learners who worked

Figure 7.9   A computing display including 'best bugs'

through their bugs, and who display an interest in where the bug was and what they had to do to correct it: they put their curiosity to use in debugging.

Starters and plenaries: a debugging workout

Plant bugs in code or algorithms and challenge learners to find these in starter or plenary activities. Who can find them first? Was this bug similar to a previous bug? You can view this as a debugging workout.

Debugging question stems

To scaffold learners' curiosity in driving them towards finding the bug, have a selection of question stems in your learning space, such as those recommended by Barefoot Computing (http://barefootcas.org.uk):

What should.......... do? Why?

What does.............do? How do you know?

Where might the bug be? Why do you think this?

What are you going to change? Why?

Curiosity in computing ... is about computational thinking across the curriculum

In Chapter 1, one theory presented of curiosity was that it is an innate drive; it comes from within us and is something we need to satisfy. After spending any time with young children and witnessing their near constant barrage of 'why' questions, it is hard not to agree. Much of these 'why' questions are aimed at the physical world around them, young children want explanations; without realising it, they are natural scientists. The science chapters of this book explore fully the relationship between curiosity and science. Here, we'll consider how learners' computational thinking skills can help foster their scientific curiosity. While we are moving away from working with computers here, as discussed in Chapter 6 the development of learners' computational thinking skills is a key aspect of the computing curriculum, and one which has far reaching benefits across the curriculum. In the case study below we'll explore how computational thinking helps learners design and undertake science investigations, enabling them to answer the questions their own scientific curiosity has brought about.

CASE STUDY

Creating superhero sunglasses

STEM link to science

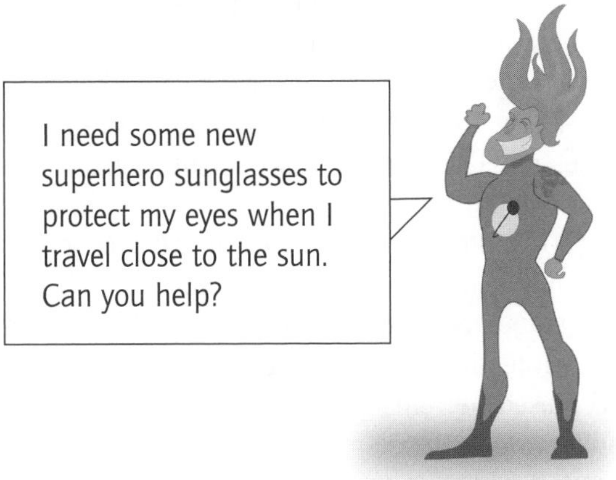

(Continued)

(Continued)

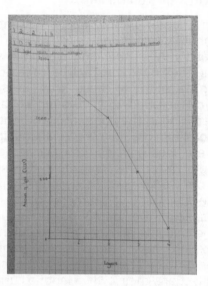

STEM link
to
mathematics

Figure 7.10 Pupils conducting a scientific enquiry and a graph of their results

In this case study, pupils were given a range of materials to construct superhero sunglasses. Learners were given time to explore the materials and came up with a scientific question to investigate: 'How will the number of layers of plastic affect the amount of light that passes through?' Learners could be seen holding several layers to classroom lights and windows (if re-creating this experiment discuss the danger of looking at the sun) trying to gauge how it affected the amount of light blocked (Figure 7.10). They decided to conduct a scientific enquiry to answer their question; let's look at how computational thinking helped with this scientific enquiry.

Turner et al. (2013) break the science enquiry process down into three stages: plan, do and review. Computational thinking skills were valuable at the planning stage, as learners decomposed the investigation down into steps and wrote the logical sequence of steps – the algorithm. Pupils also recognised patterns in the experimental process (measuring the light passing through the plastic, adding a layer and repeating), and similarly recognised a pattern of what must be kept the same each time a measurement was taken to ensure a fair test. Furthermore, as pupils conduct a range of different types of science enquiries throughout school, such as observations over time or fair tests, they will recognise a pattern in the characteristics of each type. As part of their plan, learners made a prediction, which should be a 'logical prediction' drawing upon their existing understanding to reason about their ideas.

Once learners had undertaken their experiment, computational thinking helped them analyse their results and draw sound conclusions from their work. Could they spot a pattern in the results? How does the amount of light vary with increasing layers? Once learners have identified this pattern, they can draw a logical conclusion to their investigation: *The more layers of coloured plastic you have, the more light is blocked.*

This case study illustrates how computational thinking plays a part in helping learners solve an enquiry generated by their own scientific curiosity. Loewenstein's (1994) model of curiosity highlights that learning stokes our curiosity. When we are curious about something and satisfy that curiosity, it is likely to spawn further ideas and questions, as we strive to further develop our knowledge. That was certainly the case here, when immediately learners started asking how things would differ if the plastic were a different colour, or if there was a gap between layers, or if the lens was a different size or shape. Here, computational thinking skills are helping to make learners more effective scientists. In doing so we are hopefully encouraging learners to be more curious since we are empowering them with the skills to enjoy the pleasurable experience of satisfying that curiosity as they are better able to answer the scientific questions they ask of the world.

Conclusion

This chapter has presented a range of case studies which illustrate how we can develop curious learners in computing. A key theme has been the link between curiosity and creativity, and the importance of projects allowing learners to be led by their ideas wherever this may take them, within reason. Enabling this creative approach undoubtedly requires a stronger breadth and depth of subject knowledge in us as teachers. This is why organisations providing free and low-cost, high-quality CPD such as Computing at School (www.computingatschool.com) and Barefoot Computing (www.barefootcas.org.uk) are recommended.

A second key theme has been that of sparking learners' curiosity. As computing is still in its infancy in schools, we are in the wonderful position of encouraging learners to think about things they had perhaps previously not considered and offer them new educational experiences. Indeed, many teachers may not have considered concepts such as the difference between the World Wide Web and the Internet before, and so we can share the experience of our learners, being curious together.

At present computers are not intelligent; they don't have moods, act differently on different days or feel more or less creative first thing in the morning or last thing at night: they are purely logical devices which do exactly as we tell them. As such, it is curious minds that have given us innovations, not the technology itself, and it is only curious minds that will make the most of them. It is hoped that this chapter along with Chapter 6 has provided you with an understanding of how to help your learners develop curious minds in the context of computing, and that can leave you with a sense of curiosity about what technological innovations they might go on to create.

Chapter summary

Having read this chapter you will:

- know about the wealth of resources available and specifically about a selection of resources suited to enhancing curiosity in computing in primary schools;
- have a developing understanding of the aspects of computing which enhance learners' curiosity;
- have ideas about how to plan computing lessons which enhance learners' curiosity.

CHAPTER 8

CURIOSITY IN PRIMARY DESIGN AND TECHNOLOGY

DESIGN IS A FUNNY WORD. SOME PEOPLE THINK DESIGN MEANS HOW IT LOOKS. BUT OF COURSE, IF YOU DIG DEEPER, IT'S REALLY HOW IT WORKS.

STEVE JOBS (1996)

Chapter objectives

After reading this chapter you will:

- understand the importance of curiosity in design and technology;
- know which aspects of design and technology are most influenced by curiosity;
- see how teachers can enable curiosity in pupils;
- appreciate a wide range of ways to develop curiosity in design and technology.

Overview

This chapter will explore how learners confidently build and display curious behaviours through the exploration of artefacts, e.g. when designing, exploring the strength and aesthetics of materials, observing how things work or taste, and how they are assembled. It will reference the National Curriculum (DfE, 2013) and the characteristics of design and technology. Ideas will be considered from the psychology of learning, e.g. schema, when learners start to display curiosity through exploration (Piaget, 1952; Athey, 2007; McLeod, 2015). Consideration will be given to the design process (Figure 8.3) alongside Kimbell et al.'s (1991) interaction of hand and mind (Figure 8.4) and how these ideas support our understanding of the learning processes in design and technology. This and the following chapter include illustrative STEM projects centring on design and technology, each identifying opportunities which encourage curiosity among primary age learners.

Two design technologists

> We were lucky enough to grow up in an environment where there was always much encouragement to children to pursue intellectual interests; to investigate whatever aroused curiosity.
> Orville Wright (1943) (Crouch, 2002)

If a child picked up a piece of rock from the floor to use as a toy, how might the child make the toy fly? She or he might hold it in the air and run with it. But what happens if they launch it? The toy might be thrown through the air and land nearby. A curious child might stick leaves or feathers to the rock. Another might sellotape pieces of wood to the top to look like wings. Curiosity encourages the child to build and improve, adapting their toy into something far more meaningful. It could take the child minutes or months to realise that the rock is heavy and they need a lighter material or more force. Perhaps a catapult mechanism is required to slingshot the toy higher into the air? Curiosity has the potential to drive the development of a better artefact from its earlier simple beginning.

STEM link to science

Now take this on a step. How might one construct a craft in which people can sit and fly? What would be the success criteria? A vehicle strong enough to hold the passengers, powerful enough to get from A to B. There are a number of criteria required for an object to become an aircraft. It must be heavier than air, take off, fly and land under its own power and must be controllable along all three axes (known as roll, pitch, yaw). Although history

STEM link to mathematics

Figure 8.1   The Wright brothers

debates whether the Wright brothers (Figure 8.1) were the first to fly a plane, their wing warping design and continued research and development meant that they were the first to design a successful commercially viable aeroplane that had powered, controlled, sustained flight.

Their curiosity started with research into vehicles that could fly without an engine. In 1899 they conducted a literature review into all current aeronautical research done so far. Selecting highly suitable timber from a Giant spruce for the construction, they developed the mechanism that could laterally control a fixed wing. In 1903, the Kitty Hawk made its debut flight and by 1908 through refinement and further refinement, the brothers secured their place as pioneers of flight, demonstrating the successful tight turns their invention could perform, and out-performing any competition. So where has this curiosity in developing aviation taken us a century later? There are somewhere between one and two million people in the air at any one time with the largest aircraft carrying over 700 passengers; we have developed craft that fly seven times the speed of sound (Figure 8.2), and the well-known Boeing 747 is built with around seven million parts. The curiosity of the Wright brothers has influenced how as a world nation we travel, work, holiday, import and export food and goods, and provide emergency support.

Figure 8.2 The NASA x43-a

Why is curiosity important in design and technology?

To understand curiosity in primary design and technology we must first define design and technology in education. In the context of primary school learners, the Design and Technology Association (DATA) (2015) summarises:

> *Design and Technology gives children the opportunity to develop skill, knowledge and understanding of designing and making functional products ... it is vital to nurture creativity and innovation through design, and by exploring the designed and made world in which we all live and work.*

Design and technology projects require clear design briefs based perhaps on four key elements. The learners will design and make:

- an artefact or system;
- for an identified user or client;
- for a particular purpose;
- with the criteria for a good product in mind.

Reflective activity:

Which of the following are genuine design and technology projects? (adapted from Ofsted, 2013a)

Building a replica of the Eiffel Tower.

Making a shelter for the Teddy Bears' Picnic.

Painting a portrait of Queen Elizabeth II.

Designing a moving vehicle to transport water around a room.

Making a healthy sandwich for your class picnic.

Building a model of a volcano.

The shelter, vehicle and sandwich activities above were all genuine design and technology projects because DT involves thinking about what products are used for and the needs of those who use them. Modelling, drawing or using certain types of 2D or 3D materials do not in themselves make an activity design and technology' (Ofsted, 2013a). A good design and technology education activity has to have sufficient depth and breadth to enable pupils to learn practical skills, provide them with the knowledge to make products that satisfy the design brief, and are safe and healthy. Pupils need to be able to test, refine and develop the products they design and make, to check them and improve them if they can.

Skills in design and technology that are linked to/draw out curiosity

Skill development from the Early Years to Key Stage 2 and beyond

A curious young hand extends out towards a desired item; the child wants to hold it, feel it, taste it and explore it. Children are curious about what a new object is, for everything in the world is new, exciting and a potential learning experience. Very young learners will opt to use their mouth to explore at every opportunity. This is sensory learning. What sound does the object make if it is banged on a table? What happens if it is shaken?

What happens if it is dropped? These are forms of exploratory learning. The mouth and nose are vital sense organs for a curious one-year-old, and understanding is developed using all the senses. At two years old the child has normally moved away from putting things in their mouth and prefers to explore manually. Gross motor skills are developed enough to generally manipulate hand-held items. Through observation, commonalities can be seen to develop through play and are known as types of schema (Piaget, 1952). 'It is useful to think of schemas as "units" of knowledge, each relating to one aspect of the world, including objects, actions and abstract (i.e. theoretical) concepts' (McLeod, 2015). Children will start to discover how to build items and knock them down, and will try to put things inside other items (enclosure/container), underneath them (enveloping) or align them (Athey, 2007).

During infancy and early childhood, children develop through a number of schema, some lasting days, others lasting months. It is through these that a child tests and retests conditions; they are natural, uncontrollable and necessary urges that all children have. Other schemas include rotation, orientation, trajectory, positioning, connection, transporting and transformation (Caro, 2012). As infants develop they want to know what can be done; can the object be pulled apart to look inside? Can it be rebuilt or items used to make their project bigger or better? Can items be lined up neatly, can order be created? He or she will begin to create projects using random available items such as using glue, Sellotape and/or ties. The curious mind of a child entering Reception class becomes much more sophisticated; they want to make something that has purpose. For example, would a teddy bear like a tent? Can they utilise a blanket? How will they fix the blanket to make a tent? They begin to consider the aesthetics of the item (borrowing flowers and glitter to decorate it) and its function (a sleeping bag made out of a tea towel and a sponge wrapped in cloth for a pillow lead to further questions, such as, is it warm enough for teddy?). Self-directed projects are amended, adjusted and improved to develop meaningful products. This can be followed by stories created by the child about why the product is needed (purpose) and what it can be used for (intended user).

With encouragement and opportunity, curiosity will flourish. If we are allowed to explore objects with our hands as well as gather detail with our other senses, if we are allowed to explore the great outdoors whatever the weather, and have the freedom to make mistakes whatever the project, we can learn many skills that can support our development into adulthood. An advocate of this method of experimental and experiential learning was Bruner who explained that important outcomes of learning include not just the concepts, categories and problem-solving procedures invented previously by the culture, but also the ability to 'invent' these things for oneself (McLeod, 2008).

Through our curiosity in design and technology we have the opportunity to learn how to overcome hurdles, to learn about resilience. If something doesn't work the first time, we have learned something, so now we can change it. We learn about persistence; if it doesn't look like our original idea, we adapt it. We become critical of our own work and identify ways in which we would like to improve on our design.

In the Early Years curriculum, STEM subjects are placed in specific areas of learning and development as explained in the Early Years Statutory Framework (2014). Design and technology comes under the umbrella of 'Understanding the world,' alongside the primary subjects 'computing' and 'science'. Thus, the Early Years Foundation Stage already has some integration of STEM subjects. Other main headings include 'numeracy' and 'expressive arts and design', both areas which lend themselves to STEM development. Cross-thematic activities are planned both indoors and outdoors underpinned by the characteristics of effective learning.

Key phrases within the Early Years guidance illustrate perfectly how good practice within this age group continues through meaningful projects in Key Stage 1 and Key Stage 2. It states that children should work with projects that are open-ended resulting from innate curiosity, building concepts, testing ideas and finding out. That playfulness comes from combining, refining and exploring ideas in imaginative ways, considering other perspectives. Curious learners develop resilience in their learning through a 'can do' attitude, seeking new challenges, taking risks and seeing failures as opportunities. Attention, persistence and enjoying achieving what they set out to do help to support long-term success. Through the design process they will make links using what they already know with links to new concepts to support choices and decision making.

Imagineering and the design cycle

Imagineering is a term used in design and technology; it refers to the use of the imagination to envisage solutions and then engineering a solution. We can, perhaps, all imagine a bucket made of jelly. Can you imagine buckets made of other more suitable materials? Can you imagine different sized or shaped buckets?

Can you imagine improvement on the basic bucket design? Perhaps a spout? A lid? A different handle? Another feature? Such imagineering is a very useful skill in design and technology. This process may be a form of curiosity enabling design and technologists to pose questions such as:

- will it work?
- will the user value it?
- can we make it more appealing?
- is it safe?
- is it strong enough for the user?
- does it do what we want it to do?

This can be interesting to observe in the primary classroom. More skills are observed as learners negotiate stages in the so-called design and make cycle (see Figure 8.3). Some may focus mainly on the function, e.g. how can we make it go faster? Shall we add more batteries? Can we put lights on it? How can we make it go further? Other learners will be more focused on the form or finish, e.g. is the shape pleasing? What about adding some glitter and feathers? Will the user like ours the best?

This cyclic process is one which the learner may repeat a number of times with the aim of refining their project as they get closer to the desired final result. We can see curiosity contributing

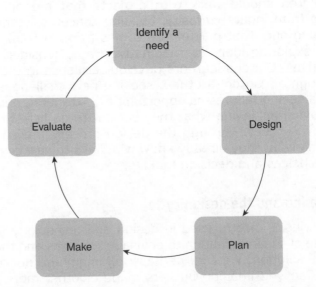

Figure 8.3 A model of design and technology – the design and make cycle

to each stage – for example, the human need for solutions is all around us. Curious minds spot these and often begin to wonder about options, different materials, shapes, forms, functions. Kimbell et al. (1991) suggested an alternative but in some ways complementary iterative process between hand and mind (see Figure 8.4).

Kimbell et al. (1991) emphasised an iterative process where the hand and mind interact, but where activity may be led by one or the other. The toing and froing of the hand and mind gives the learner the opportunity to think, act and think again. Although the iterative process shows a clear directional path from design brief to product, those observing young learners in the primary classroom see them flitting back and forth within this and not necessarily in a structured, orderly manner (for example, they may get the brief, think of an idea, draw up a plan, experience artefacts and go straight back to the draw-ing board before implementation). This is similar in a number of ways to the tinkering referred to in Chapters 6 and 7 on computing.

Bricolage (French for making things with materials which hap-pen to be available) is used to describe two processes which are relevant to the design process. The first is in the way we learn by improvisation of materials; for example, through bricolage both the materials and the learner transform what was once two chairs and a bed-sheet into a house in which children can

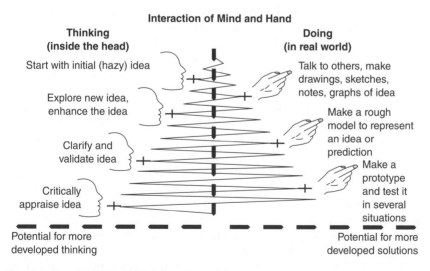

Figure 8.4   Iteration of hand and mind in design and technology (from Kimbell et al. 1991)

play at being parents (Sharples et al., 2013). The second use of the term in education relates to engaging in innovation by creative exploration of the practices and technologies needed to achieve an educational goal. It is about trying things, developing and testing, and learning from mistakes. This is very similar to tinkering and shows clear links to curiosity – evident in the STEM subjects.

The programme of study for design and technology (DfE, 2013) does not explicitly refer to curiosity; it does, however, require that learners examine the function and form of a range of existing products. It encourages learners to be curious about the way that things are made. It makes several explicit references to creativity which is akin to and which is fuelled by curiosity. The subject aims of the curriculum in design and technology (DfE, 2013) assert that all pupils should:

- develop the creative, technical and practical expertise needed to perform everyday tasks confidently and to participate successfully in an increasingly technological world;
- build and apply a repertoire of knowledge, understanding and skills in order to design and make high-quality prototypes and products for a wide range of users;
- critique, evaluate and test their ideas and products and the work of others;
- understand and apply the principles of nutrition and learn how to cook.

Creativity is driven by curious minds and curious hands. Creativity in a primary classroom can be defined as 'discovering things new to us, making things that we never made before, and bringing our very own interpretation to the world around us' (Lieberman, 2014). A powerful driving force for creativity is a curious mind, one which views the world with questioning curious eyes.

Another model of the design in design and technology imagines special glasses through which we view the world in a designerly way. The idea of design glasses has assisted some learners in that the imaginary design and technology spectacles focuses the attention on design. They might ask, why was that material used? Is that the most suitable shape/arrangement/pattern? Older learners might start this process by drawing annotated sketches, cross-sectional and exploded diagrams to plan their design. In Key Stage 1, discussion and simple sketches or modelling can start the design process.

Being curious in design and technology might see learners pose questions such as:

- is X the best material for Y?
- if I changed X would it be better/faster/warmer/tastier?
- if I see X in nature could I copy this?
- how does this work?
- how are things made/assembled?
- what design would fulfill the brief?
- would a change in X affect the result?
- would my user like my design?
- does my design really fit the brief to the best it can?
- can I make it even better? If so, how?

A design and technology curious classroom

We recognise a classroom like this when we observe young learners confident to have a go, not afraid of errors, knowing that they can learn from mistakes. These children have a growing confidence in their skills and knowledge around and dealing with materials, and processes. They relish contexts in which they have to consider a problem or design brief, account for the needs of the user and develop a product utilising the materials and skills at their disposal. Thus, in a design and technology curious classroom contexts are sought and exploited which allow young hands and minds to explore, question and produce solutions. The following examples demonstrate this.

So how do we spark this curiosity in design technology? The question or challenge we set ourselves or our learners must be engaging, challenging, appropriate and fun. It needs a clear purpose. What is it for? The user must be identified. Who is it for? This design process is not always straightforward. Part of the challenge of design and technology is working in an iterative way to make and remake, and make even better. Encouraging playfulness will assist most learners; can they play with an artefact, material or idea? These behaviours are linked to tinkering and bricolage by just playing with or exploring an idea.

A useful starting point for design and technology is the examination of existing artefacts; this is a requirement of the English National Curriculum for design and technology (DfE, 2013). Learners about to construct head torches for Harry Potter or an astronaut might first examine existing torches to see how other people have constructed them (see Figures 8.5 and 8.6). They might later be challenged to design and make an improved design. Learners might initially examine the shape and form of a series of torches prior to disassembling them to see how they work and how they were constructed.

STEM link to science

Figure 8.5 Key Stage 2 learners identify the components in a torch

Figure 8.6 Key Stage 2 children examine the functioning of existing torches

This approach is explicitly encouraging curiosity. Learners might be asked to:

- describe the form and function of a product;
- suggest why these materials, parts and shapes were chosen;
- explain how it works;
- suggest how the product was assembled.

There are times in design and technology when the work becomes very challenging for learners. Materials we have available are not always ideal. Weak structures can break and at these times learners need resilience. Curiosity and determination to find things out and to solve a problem become important to bolster resilient design and technologists.

 Reflective activity

Consider a time when you have tried to make something and failed. Did it stop you? Or were you all the more determined? Did you display resilience? What skills and qualities did you draw upon to have another go? How did you feel once you had overcome this hurdle? So from this, how can you encourage resilience in the children in your care?

CASE STUDY

Starting from children's literature

Anna's Amazing Multi-coloured Glasses by Wendy Body (1999) is a good example of how children's literature can be used as a context for curiosity in design and technology. In the story Anna finds a pair of glasses at the bottom in her garden. Through them she starts to see things differently. When she puts them on she discovers that they are magical. Every day she sees things in a different colour and new friends appear.

(Continued)

(Continued)

In the design and technology brief Anna would like to take her best friend Suzi with her on her adventures but only has one pair of glasses. The challenge for the young learners is to design a pair of amazing glasses for Suzi so she can also see the world in lots of colours and join Anna on her adventures.

The National Curriculum (DfE, 2013) requires learners to design purposeful, functional, appealing products for themselves and other users based on design criteria, working with a range of materials to make an appealing product that is fit for purpose (or an individual). To do this, the learner may require a number of skills including the use of tools to accurately cut, shape, join and finish; and research will be required to look at existing glasses designs. Cross-curricular science knowledge of transparent materials and filters will also be essential to create a meaningful product fit for purpose.

STEM link to science

Figure 8.7 Learners imagine a fantasy world through Suzi's spectacles

STEM link to mathematics

A number of links to other areas of the curriculum can promote this curiosity and the use of the learners' design even further. For example, links to numeracy singing days of the week songs and identifying shapes and colours; links to literacy using hot seating techniques and drama when Anna and Suzi enter a new environment and diary writing to describe what the characters can see.

This project encourages the curious young learner to consider what the world would look like through magical glasses. Each day Anna sees something new and amazing through her glasses and by designing a pair for a friend the learner has the opportunity to consider the shape and size of the glasses they will make, material type and colour and filter colour. Learners will need to consider a safe material that can be cut to fit the face and strong enough not to bend. They will need to consider the aesthetics of the glasses. Will Suzi want to wear them? Through research of coloured filters they can enhance the design to be more believable. They can test the light filters numerically with a torch and light meter.

STEM link to mathematics

STEM link to science

Design and technology is perhaps the most cross-curricular subject so contexts like the one above allow teachers and children to explore the made world across all disciplines. Learners are given open-ended contexts which allow play, experimentation, and trial and error. Learners are introduced to new tools and materials through engaging contexts which allow both the design and the technology to be planned for in a creative and curious manner.

CASE STUDY

Anglo-Saxons at war

To encourage curiosity in design and technology learners need to examine familiar and less familiar artefacts and systems. They need to examine them with curious eyes and look past the familiar shapes and materials asking why and how. Why was that material, shape, component, system used? How do these elements come together so that the product works? How could this product be developed?

A study of Anglo-Saxons in a Year 5/6 class is an example of how history can be used as a context for curiosity in design and technology (Figures 8.8 and 8.9). In this project the study of artefacts was essential in supporting the young learners' understanding of natural and man-made materials used in this period of history. The challenge for these curious learners was to build their own small-scale

STEM link to science

(Continued)

(Continued)

war weapon, which following production would be used in a series of competitions to see which group had made the most effective model.

The National Curriculum (DfE, 2013) requirements for Key Stage 2 provide further challenge for curious learners who must also apply their understanding of how to strengthen, stiffen and reinforce more complex structures, and understand and use mechanical systems in their products. In Figure 8.9 we can see that curiosity has led one design and technologist to create a catapult system using a cantilever, spring and pulley system to launch the payload.

Figure 8.8   An Anglo-Saxon war weapon

Figure 8.9   Larger-scale model of an Anglo-Saxon war weapon

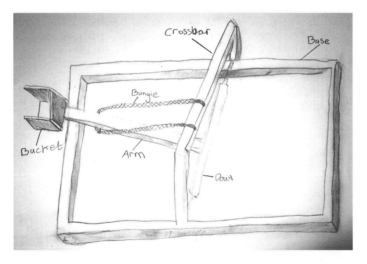

Figure 8.10   An annotated sketch of the planned design

(Continued)

In all design and technology projects, the evaluation is an essential part of the process. The National Curriculum states that learners should 'critique, evaluate and test their ideas and products and the work of others' (DFE, 2013). This in itself is a skill. Without guidance some learners may jump to simple comparison of aspects of their work to those of others. However, with design success criteria and a carefully planned evaluation which scaffolds the learners' thoughts on their experiences, learners can have a fantastic opportunity to engage in reflection, suggest future action, in order to design, plan, make and evaluate. Evaluation is perhaps the critical element from which we learn in design and technology education. Evaluation has the potential to drive curiosity even further. If our product has shortcomings how can we improve it? If our product is excellent, can it be improved?

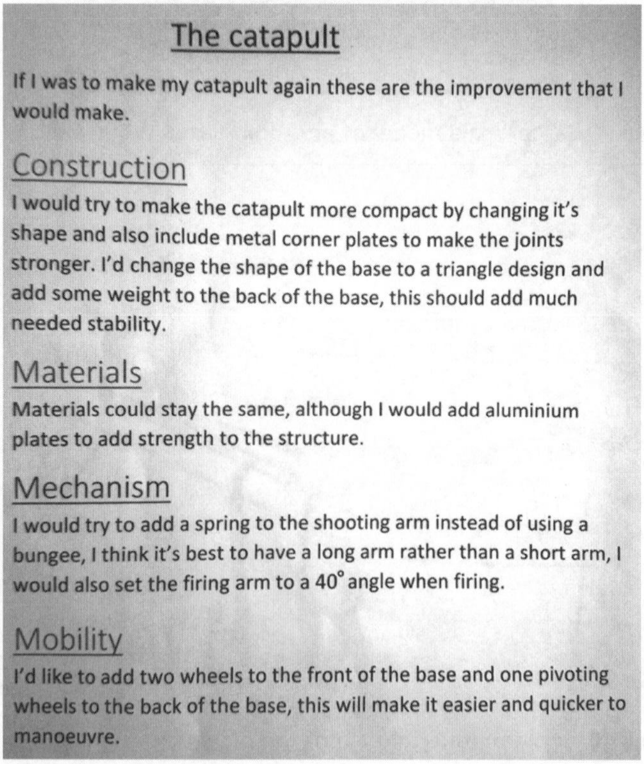

The catapult

If I was to make my catapult again these are the improvement that I would make.

Construction

I would try to make the catapult more compact by changing it's shape and also include metal corner plates to make the joints stronger. I'd change the shape of the base to a triangle design and add some weight to the back of the base, this should add much needed stability.

Materials

Materials could stay the same, although I would add aluminium plates to add strength to the structure.

Mechanism

I would try to add a spring to the shooting arm instead of using a bungee, I think it's best to have a long arm rather than a short arm, I would also set the firing arm to a 40° angle when firing.

Mobility

I'd like to add two wheels to the front of the base and one pivoting wheels to the back of the base, this will make it easier and quicker to manoeuvre.

Figure 8.11   Catapult evaluation

In the catapult example, healthy competition of each creator's war machines was used as a method to test their effectiveness. Learners were encouraged to evaluate their own and others' designs. Figure 8.11 above clearly demonstrates the evaluative process where not only are the merits of the design considered but also how this can be furthered. Sakichi Toyoda, an employee of Toyota Motor Corporation formally developed the theory of '5 whys' when he evaluated methodologies in manufacturing. In this iterative interrogative process, asking the question 'why?' five times can often get to the root cause of a design problem.

Resilience can also be required when things go wrong. Things don't always work, design and technology projects can take time, and they can require stages of work leading to a prototype of product. When learners see the subject as one of inventiveness, of creativity, they may find it more acceptable that design and technology is a journey and that curiosity will help them embrace the challenges as they arise.

 Reflective activity

When has your own evaluation of a design led you to curiosity and then action to improve the design? Has this occurred with food? With textiles? With construction materials? Perhaps you have made a dish and felt something was missing. How did you solve this problem? Did curiosity to find the missing ingredient come from trial and error? Was it the result of tinkering or from further informed research?

Conclusion

This chapter has looked at the potential in design and technology education for the development and employment of curiosity. It considered the developing child and how, through effective scaffolding, curiosity can be encouraged through playfulness and exploration. It has considered methods of design: the design cycle, the iterative model and the skills that are developed in a design project. Design and technology skills were seen to enable curiosity including physical skills, communication skills and those required to identify what is needed to develop a project. These link to important personal attributes of curiosity, creativity, persistence, decision making, rising to a challenge, and a risk-taking can-do attitude. Design and technology along with the other STEM subjects present the ideal context for the development of a wide range of knowledge, understanding and skills. Chapter 1 recognised that sometimes curiosity can lead us down the wrong path. However, in primary education we might recognise what C. J. Cherryh (1995) noted: 'Ignorance killed the cat; curiosity was framed!'

The next chapter will look at practical ways to enhance curiosity in design and technology. It will celebrate real examples taken from a number of schools where curiosity is channelled through exciting projects which harness motivation; where learners are encouraged to speculate about 'what if ...?' and develop their ideas from a carefully designed brief to promote the very best in engagement, motivation and thinking.

Chapter summary

Having read the chapter you will:

- be clear about how curiosity can be enhanced through design and technology;
- understand how child development encourages curiosity in the world around them;
- understand that curiosity has considerable value to learners and the learning of each STEM subject.

CHAPTER 9

WAYS TO ENHANCE CURIOSITY IN PRIMARY DESIGN AND TECHNOLOGY

Chapter objectives

After reading this chapter you will:

- have a strongly developing understanding of how curiosity impacts on learning in design and technology;
- be able to see how the key elements of a successful design project can enable curiosity;
- identify how, through authentic design projects, curiosity can lead to creativity and innovation in young learners.

Overview

In the last chapter the key elements of a design and technology project were determined: that a user is identified, and that the product has a clear purpose when designing and making a product. Igniting the learner's curiosity through open-ended enquiry, and design through the iterative design cycle were linked to Kimbell et al.'s (1991) hand and mind model. The notion of tinkering and flitting were used to support our understanding of how a curious young learner develops their understanding through the study of artefacts and through research to create a design. Bruner's theories on learning (1957) explained that experimental and experiential learning will enable learners to look 'beyond the data to new and possibly fruitful predictions', so children may take what they already know to be out there and through curiosity and determination it will drive them to create something meaningful for themselves.

In this second chapter about curiosity in design and technology we review and reflect on successful examples in the primary classroom which help us to articulate what we mean by curiosity in this subject. We look at successful starting points of a project and make links to other areas of the curriculum which may enrich learners' experiences. We will consider meaningful contexts and how a learner's curiosity and self-determination motivates them to find a solution to a challenge. The importance of team work and how the curiosity of a team bring together different perspectives, a collective of ideas, and a shared mind approach will be discussed, alongside the role of the teacher and how they may help to promote creativity and curiosity rather than, as mentioned in Chapter 1, 'killing it'.

Promoting curiosity in design and technology is ...?

This section considers pedagogical approaches that can help to cultivate and maintain levels of curiosity in design and technology.

Curiosity in design and technology is about ...
open-ended opportunity

A distinctive characteristic of good design and technology education is the open-ended nature of tasks and challenges. They can provide very rich experiences which require, enable and strengthen curiosity in learners.

CASE STUDY

A winter-warm fairy

This case study illustrates a creative open-ended activity aimed at upper Key Stage 2. The stimulus for this project is fantasy worlds. Learners are challenged to design something to keep a fairy warm in winter.

The National Curriculum (DfE, 2013) requires learners to work with a range of materials to make an appealing product that is fit for purpose (or an individual). To do this, the learner may require a number of skills including the use of tools to accurately cut, shape, join and finish. In upper Key Stage 2 this should involve a number of steps to complete the design, applying a range of finishing techniques. Cross-curricular science knowledge of insulating materials will also be essential to create a meaningful product fit for purpose.

DATA (2013) agreed that that there are six interrelated principles which may be useful to support each stage of the design process. We can take the design brief of the winter fairy needing help to keep warm to aid our understanding of these six principles:

'User'

Curiosity for the learner comes from investigating the needs of the user. What would they want, what would interest/excite them? What would be their viewpoint and of value to them? In this design brief, would the fairy like warm clothes? A waterproof suit? Or shall we build a shelter underground? A tree house to fly into? When learners are working in a group, a collective of ideas has already begun. The possibilities and the suitability of each may be discussed. These ideas are like pebbles skimming the surface of a body of water. Some ideas will sink immediately, and some will cause ripples, whereas one or two ideas will cause waves of excitement. Considering the potential of these possibilities magnifies the curiosity of the collaborators and informal feedback within the group can be highly motivating.

'Purpose'

Careful consideration of the product and its objective. Curiosity comes from considering the research the learner(s) will need to 'do a proper job'. How will the design work? What features will it need to keep the fairy warm? A culture of child as maker or 'maker culture' (Sharples, et. al, 2013) emphasises experimentation, innovation and the testing of theory through practical, self-directed tasks to create a product which suits the user's purpose.

(Continued)

(Continued)

'Design Decisions'

What shall we make? What will it look like? What will it do? The curious learner will develop their knowledge of artefacts and learning in other subjects to demonstrate their creative, technical and practical expertise. They will make meaningful links to their current knowledge, e.g. what clothes do I wear in winter? How is our home warmer in winter than in summer? What do we do differently in the winter season to keep warm? They will further this understanding by making links to science and nature – for example considering which materials are the best insulators. They will be curious about how they can join materials together to create a quality product; and how it could be appealing to the user. A shared-mind approach will ensure the features are acceptable by all members if in group-work.

STEM link to science

'Innovation'

The open-ended opportunities provided in this project example ensure the curious learner has an opportunity to be original, to draw out and discuss a number of ideas, leading to originality. The classroom will not have 15 prototypes of the same item, but meaningful solutions that have been driven by curiosity to solve the fairy's problem. Young learners should be encouraged by the teacher and their peers to take risks, to explore new and novel techniques to further their skills. Through the iterative design cycle and the notion of tinkering, young learners can build on their resilience through a fail-safe culture where mistakes are celebrated as part of the design process.

'Authenticity'

Products should be believable, real and meaningful to the curious learner and others. By allowing them the opportunity to consider a number of solutions and make something that they believe to be the most suitable through study and research of artefacts, the learner has completed the first round of the design cycle. If the evaluation includes an opportunity to plan improvements with reflection on why this change should be made to their product, then the learner has entered double-loop learning as described by Argyris and Schon (1978).

Figure 9.1   Textiles activity: construction of a winter-warm fairy

An important decision to make as a teacher is how much do we want the learner to complete a task that fits the curriculum objectives you have planned, or can they make whatever they see fit to answer the brief? Is it important that the learners all make an item of clothing or they all make a shelter? Consider which would embrace the learner's curiosity the most. The National Curriculum (DfE, 2013) guides you to create opportunities (in textiles and structures) throughout each key stage to design, make and evaluate using a range of developing skills. Nowhere does it say that all learners should make the same thing at the same time. Is inventiveness the thing here? If the learner perceives a problem in the world and asks the question how can we solve this problem? Should it then be that the educator gives the learner the tools and knowledge to support this inventiveness?

Now consider the Early Years Foundation Stage: the characteristics of effective learning suggest that best practice includes activities where learners are playing and exploring, active learning, and creating and thinking critically. Therefore, practitioners may suggest an activity when providing resources but it is the curiosity of the learner that decides ultimately on what those resources will make. Early learners are natural tinkerers; they can decide on their own design brief, they create their own success criteria and they may go round the

(Continued)

(Continued)

design and make cycle (Figure 8.3, see page 140) a number of times, with or without adult support. Curiosity can flourish when activity is open-ended, it is not limited to design and technology, but may include mathematics, science, computing, art, or indeed any other area of the curriculum if the learning experience is meaningful to the curious young learner.

 Reflective activity

What are your experiences of design and technology? Do you hold the need for open-ended challenge in high regard? Were you allowed this freedom as a young learner or constrained to a specific prototype? If curiosity is a driving factor in designing authentic products, then let us consider the role of the teacher. Look at the following verbs – which enable curiosity and which may stifle it?

Do, tell, enable, support, advise, stand-back, supply, inform, encourage, withhold, demonstrate, change, teach, provide, give.
    Is it what we do or how we do it?

Curiosity in design and technology is about …
developing meaningful contexts

CASE STUDY

Dirty Gertie's birthday party

Children's literature presents many contexts which learners find relevant, in this case the need is for healthy food choices. Learners empathise with the character in the story and are able to relate to/reflect on their own past experiences adding coherence. In this case the project is aimed at Key Stage 1, challenging curious learners to design something to encourage healthy eating.

It was soon to be dirty Gertie's birthday party. "I want chocolate mummy! And pizza, and hotdogs, and burgers, and super sour sweeties that make my tongue fizz and my head feel like it's going to pop off!" exclaimed Gertie. "Really Gertie? You haven't chosen anything healthy there. I was thinking of carrot and cucumber sticks and a fruit salad?" At this, Gertie stuck her tongue out and blew the biggest, rudest raspberry she could manage. "I don't want rabbit food! It's my birthday!" Adapted from Simon, F. (2009) *Horrid Henry's Birthday Party*. London: Orion Children's Books

In the design and technology brief, the learners are asked to consider how they can encourage healthy treats at Gertie's party. Can they design a fun plate that Gertie will love? Could it possibly have five fruits or vegetables for their '5-a-day'? The National Curriculum at Key Stage 1 (DfE, 2013) requires learners to know where food comes from and prepare simple dishes that do not require cooking. To complete this particular challenge, the learner may require a number of skills including selecting, peeling, grating, cutting and arranging to create a dish that is appealing to the user and appropriate to the context. They will learn how the way they cut a fruit can change its shape or look completely. For example, cutting a lime lengthways we get a segment; cut it in half and we get a star image. Cross-curricular knowledge of healthy eating and '5-a-day' help to make the science learning relevant; and through a context that they can relate to it can be emotionally engaging for the curious learner.

The purpose of the challenge is for the learner to realise that food can be healthy as well as fun, that it can be tasty, appealing and easily prepared. They will know someone (or they themselves) may not like fruit or will be anxious about trying new foods. Food is itself highly motivating and in many cases familiar. Thus, learners have a medium, fruit and vegetables, about which they feel confident and willing to explore ideas. Learners will need to consider which foods go well together (see Figure 9.2). What type of picture will they create? A rocket? A monster? A fruit burger? Gertie's face? Presentation of food is important so they will need to consider the aesthetics of the fruit plate. Will Dirty Gertie want to eat it? Through research of how fruit has been used in art, e.g. Guiseppe Arcimboldo's Feast for the Eyes, they can enhance the design to be more believable. The number of design possibilities in this project is endless due to the open-ended starting point

STEM link to science

(Continued)

(Continued)

which engages the learners by considering what motivates them. The curiosity to make their ideas into something innovative and fun ensures each design has authenticity and is appealing to the user.

Links to other areas of the curriculum enhance the curiosity of the learner even further and give them an opportunity to immerse themselves in the context of healthy living. For example science: can we grow our own food? Which senses help us to identify what we eat and what we like? Maths: do we all like the same thing – let's make a pictogram from our research. Literacy: writing an instructional text. Art: observational drawings or printing using a range of media.

STEM link to science

STEM link to mathematics

Figure 9.2 Cooking and nutrition activity: a monster fruit face

In Key Stage 2, the National Curriculum (DfE, 2013) suggests that pupils learn how to take risks, becoming resourceful, innovative, enterprising and capable citizens; that high-quality design and technology education makes an essential contribution to the creativity, culture, wealth and well-being of the nation. Event-based learning is an ideal way of promoting curiosity through the design of something that would otherwise be seen as an 'everyday item'. Schools and local communities often hold traditions such as the Christmas and summer fayres. These bring together a wealth of potential users and give the curious learner an opportunity to be enterprising. Working towards the design of a food product that can be sold brings out the entrepreneurship of our young learners and makes links to mathematics. How much of each ingredient will we need? How much product can we make? How much profit? Preparing and cooking a variety of dishes needs careful considera-tion in a primary school where cooking resources may be limited; however, there are a number of cheap technological solutions – for example the slow cooker. Young learners may grow their own fruit and vegetables in the school grounds to create marvellous jams, chutneys, soups and stews. Having such an event as a focus gives

Figure 9.3   Bonfire casserole in a slow cooker

Figure 9.4   Blackcurrant jam made from fruit collected around the school

Figure 9.5 A DIY hot chocolate marshmallow man

learners something concrete to work towards and to reflect upon afterwards, together with a sense of personal engagement and excitement (Sharples, 2013).

Curiosity in design and technology is about … design

Design and technology is not just about designing on paper and making things. It accepts that design goes on from the start until the end of the design-and-make process. It accepts that play and playfulness is necessary with materials, tools and ideas. Tinkering, a term used in previous chapters of this book, is very much part of the world of design and technology. Design technologists tinker with elements like this to improve on the design or plan and the artefact. We might adapt its shape, form, colour, texture, mechanisms, input features, outputs and more.

Design technologists look at the world through curious, 'designerly' glasses. Take a look at the chair on the left in Figure 9.6. Can you suggest ways to improve its design?

 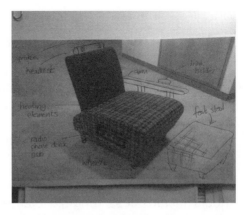

Figure 9.6 Photograph of a chair and the same photograph with drawn and annotated suggested design elements by a teacher

Based on the Creativity Wheel (Redmund, 2005), the prompts below are valuable in articulating the kinds of behaviours we might seek to see in our children. These creative designerly behaviours require and enable design and curiosity.

Promoting curiosity in design and technology is …?

Imagination with purpose

- I can see more than one way of looking at things.
- I can create things in my mind.
- I ask questions about things that could happen.
- I am able to try out new things.
- I trust my feelings about things.
- I try out lots of different ways to do things and solve problems.
- I can compare one thing to another and can make connections between different things.

Originality

- I don't always believe things just because everyone else does.
- I can find new ways to do things.
- I can think of unusual ways of doing things.
- I am prepared to try things out even if they might not work.
- I like finding out about new things and new ways of doing things.

Value

- I can use things I have already learned to help me.
- I stop and think about how I am doing in my work.
- I can spot problems and ways of dealing with them.
- I can see if my work has achieved its purpose.
- I can see how other people work to achieve their purposes.

These prompts might help teachers and children themselves understand what we mean when we talk about curiosity. Of course, as teachers we should be wary of trying to pin creativity down to a series of statements, by its very nature creativity should include less tangible elements such as visioning in our minds. Visioning for many is that mental picture we work with in our heads as we envisage a solution to a question.

Design and technology projects benefit from clarity about design briefs. It is common for teachers to provide the brief and criteria, but there is much to be gained by shifting the responsibility of this to the children. Can they examine a context, for example, a litter problem in school, and develop their own design brief? Would they need to do some research initially? By giving learners a problem, and encouraging them to come up with the solution following research, the learner begins to feel ownership of the design and technology project. It could be that this ownership drives the motivation to succeed, and allows for a true sense of pride in their product. When the responsibility of the design process is created by the learner or group of learners through a shared-mind approach, then they are able to consider their own success criteria to the brief – a rubber glove, a picking-up tool, an outdoor hoover, a rotary brush. Carefully articulated design criteria enable learning and achievement in design and technology as they focus attention and enable pairs and teams of learners to pursue a group objective.

 Reflective activity

Have you developed your own success criteria to make something? Perhaps on completion you thought...yes but it could just do with a little...If I add x it would...it would be much better if I just...Is this developing success criteria? What about sharing your design with a friend or colleague? How did you react to this advice? Did this encourage your curiosity to develop your design further?

Curiosity in design and technology is about …
exploring materials, structures and skills

CASE STUDY

A shelter from the storm

To promote design and technology education a teacher might consider how they will develop the breadth and depth of the learner's knowledge of existing artefacts and how the learner may develop sufficient practical and personal skills to construct something purposeful and meaningful. The learner needs to have opportunities to develop their own subject knowledge through the study of artefacts and technological application so they may apply this in a new challenge, and have time to evaluate, refine and re-evaluate their planned design. Earlier on in the chapter we looked at the insulating properties of materials as a focus for a design where warmth was an essential feature. In this example materials are used to shelter a person. Here, although the natural materials will provide shelter from the weather, it will be important for the learner to consider the strength and stability of the structure. Can they make joints to stop it falling down? How do they secure the leaves and branches? How can they make it comfortable? Also, spatial awareness of the size of the structure and its suitability to the number of users will need to be considered.

The National Curriculum (DfE, 2013) requires learners to select from and use a wide range of materials and components, including construction materials according to their functional properties and aesthetic qualities that are fit for purpose, aimed at particular individuals or groups. To do this, the learner requires a number of skills, applying their understanding of how to strengthen, stiffen and reinforce more complex structures using natural materials to shelter a person from a storm. Cross-curricular knowledge of natural waterproofing and insulating will also be required, and learners should evaluate their ideas and products against their own design criteria and consider the views of others to improve their work.

> STEM link to mathematics

> STEM link to science

This design brief challenges the learners into thinking about how they could provide shelter for themselves. Their curiosity will enable

(Continued)

(Continued)

their designing and making. Learners will need to consider the natural materials that are available to them. They will need to research examples of shelters and frames that will support their desired structure. How will they fasten the support together? Can they make a door? What about a window? How big does it need to be to fit their team? How small can they make it to keep them warm in their shelter? They will need to consider the aesthetics. Will it look suitable? Will it be sturdy enough for people to trust it? Will it be safe to enter it? Does it offer shelter and comfort?

Figure 9.7   A shelter

⊞   Reflective activity

Consider the necessary skills required for a successful design and technology project such as drawing, cutting, designing, making, etc. How do they enable curiosity? Is curiosity itself a design and technology skill? Or is it part of all elements of design and technology? Do these questions demonstrate curiosity?

Let us consider outdoor learning and its benefits. A government publication, *Learning outside the classroom manifesto* (DfES, 2006) highlighted its benefits in that the potential for learning is max-imised if we use the powerful combination of physical, visual and naturalistic ways of learning as well as our linguistic and math-ematical intelligence. An Ofsted report (2008) titled *Learning outside the classroom, how far should you go?* identified that the most effectively managed schools included learning outside the classroom as an integral part of a well-planned curriculum which ensured the coherent and progressive development of knowledge, skills and understanding. The emotional well-being of our young learners is also enhanced by outdoor provision, with a staggering one in ten young people being affected by mental health issues (Mental Health Foundation, 2015). Design and technology in the great outdoors offers much more than development of knowledge and skills.

Curiosity in design and technology is about …
exploring new tools

As well as providing experience of new or less familiar materials, design and technology introduces learners to new tools includ-ing, for example, a junior hacksaw, a needle threader or an App. This case study considers resources which allow design and technology to link with computers and computing.

CASE STUDY

Programmable devices

Electrical or electronic control and sensing is a very powerful facet of design and technology. It is not difficult to think of electronic and other machines in the home and workplace that use sets of instructions to perform functions, e.g. washing machines or SMART TVs. The Bee Bot© programmable toy (Figure 9. 8) is an example that is used to teach com-puting but is itself a product of design and technology. Part of design and technology is control, so teachers need simple and more complex options to control the actions of images on the screen and even better actual control mechanisms. Learners meeting Bee Bot for the first time instantly want to know more about the robot. How is it controlled? Why

STEM link
to computing

(Continued)

(Continued)

is there a hook on the back? Can they control its movement around a track? Teachers can extend the basic input of control functions to consider design and technology which makes clothing for the robot, a hat, a sleeping bag, a garage, a bridge, a roadway. Questions can be posed such as what does the unit one mean when we say forward one? What is the turn when we press the left arrow? There are links to science in terms of towing masses and friction exploring how Bee Bot© moves on different surfaces.

Figure 9.8   Bee Bot – a programmable toy

Like Bee Bot, buffer boxes allow an input and an output. If I give this instruction, what action will occur? In Figure 9.9 we see 'Learn and Go'© from Teaching Technology Systems, which is a simple buffer box or interface controlling buzzers, lights or motors. In this case a set of three lights are traffic lights and are controlled individually. Learners simply 'teach' the Bee Bot© or buffer box a sequence of on and off commands with time measured in real time and the device will simply repeat those commands.

Buffer boxes such as Flowel© provide more functionality as they are controlled by software on a computer. They allow children to control a range of lights, motors and buzzers. Their advantage is that they can

STEM link
to computing

Figure 9. 9   Learn and Go© (available from Data Harvest Group)

also sense from switches. For example, as a train approaches a level crossing it closes a switch (input), a computer program then switches on a motor to lower a barrier and activate a light, which then flashes (output) until the train passes by. As it leaves the train turns another switch so that we have another input and corresponding output, the opening of barriers and the lights being switched off.

Flowel © can operate real lights and motors (Figure 9.10) or a simulation on screen (Figure 9.11).

STEM link
to computing

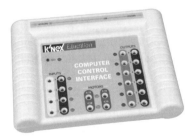 

Figure 9.10   Flowel© Buffer Box (picture provided by TTS)

(Continued)

(Continued)

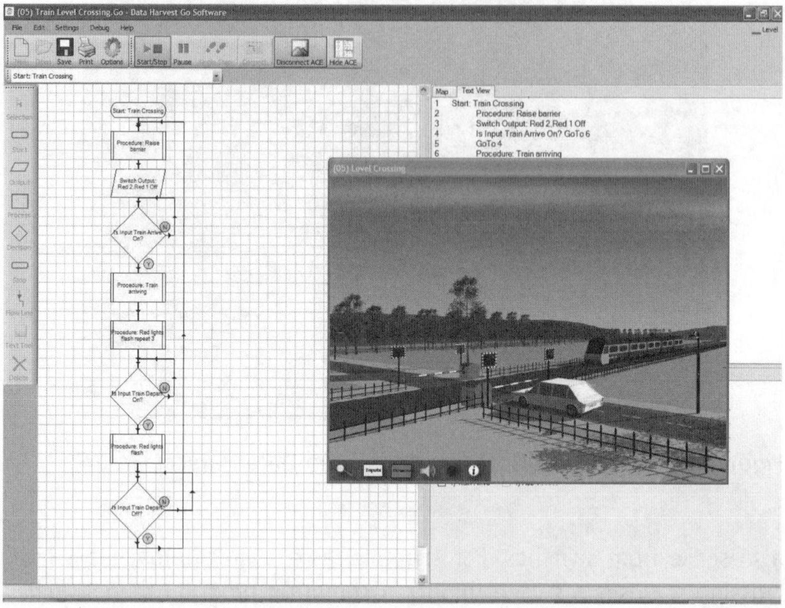

Figure 9.11 Algorythm to control a screen model of a rail crossing (picture provided by Data Harvest www.data-harvest.co.uk/catalogue/technology/primary/software/primary-software/3550)

Reflective activity

As you read about new technology, do you respond with curiosity? Do you wonder about how this could be used and applied in the world as well as in the classroom?

STEM link to computing

STEM link to computing

The opportunity for primary-aged learners to design their own switch to control a computer is provided by Makey Makey©. Any object or material can become a switch as described in Chapter 7. In Figure 9.12, we see that pasta shapes are used to allow the typing of text.

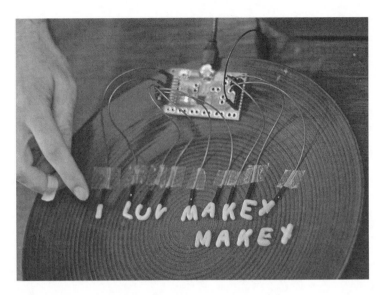

Figure 9.12   Makey Makey© allows you to design your own input devices
(picture provided by Makey Makey©)

CASE STUDY

An electronic game

The examples below show learners in a Key Stage 2 class responding to a design brief to make a game using Makey Makey©. The tinfoil lining in the game acts as a buzzer and should the player touch it, this will lead to them losing one of their three lives. In this instance, Makey Makey© was linked up to the Scratch© programme on the interactive whiteboard so the players could see their lives being lost.

> STEM link
> to computing

Figure 9.13 shows the first stage of development of a maze where the player moves a magnet from start to finish without touching the sides of the maze or traps. In Figure 9.14 we can see a different response to the same design brief where the learners have based their design from previous experience of a well-known game where parts need to be removed using tweezers.

> STEM link
> to science

(Continued)

(Continued)

Figure 9.13   Developing a Makey Makey© maze

Figure 9.14   An alternative game design

Scratch© is developed by the Lifelong Kindergarten Group at the MIT Media Lab. See http://scratch.mit.edu

Reflective activity

Can you remember a time when you designed something? Part of a garden? A flower arrangement? The layout of furniture in a classroom? A sandcastle? A classroom display? Did you form an imaginary picture in your head? Did this initiate or drive your curiosity? (Would X be possible? Would Y work? How might I achieve A or B? If I can make this happen it may be possible even to…?) Did you require resilience to create this 'something' that was meaningful to you?

Curiosity in design and technology is about …
the individual and the team

One consideration when planning a new challenge for young learners is whether they work as individuals to create their own product or as a team. Resources and timing can be a key factor in this decision and for this reason many projects seen in schools are collaborative in approach. However, it is useful to reflect on 'Maintaining curiosity in science' when considering practical work in STEM subjects (Ofsted, 2013). It warned us that group work can be a 'barrier to independent learning,' as while it may help to 'develop the [learners'] collaborative and communication skills, it risks losing independent thinking, as well as the individual mastery of the necessary manipulative and measuring skills'. It also made links to design and technology, warning us that without individual work personal initiative and independence may be curtailed, and can allow some [learners] to avoid practical manipulations altogether. Their recommendations where group work went well, were for the teacher to 'choose the groups carefully, explaining the roles of each [learner] within the group. It was suggested that a 'circus' of activities where learners may work through a series of skills through a number of lessons 'should resolve any equipment shortfall'.

Whether young learners work in groups or individually on a design, it is the time given for exploration and tinkering, the time to learn and practise new skills that enable curiosity to flourish. Considering the limitations felt by the learner in evaluations, it is often the word 'time' or 'not enough time' that is a key limitation in creativity and curiosity.

Conclusion

Curiosity is at the heart of design and technology, which is all about the way we devise systems and products to meet our needs or the needs of others. As teachers, we need to be aware of the contribution of curiosity to design and technology so that we can enable the natural curiosity of children to explore and interact with the world including the designed and made world. Exploration of artefacts, research of technologies, tinkering time, developing their own design brief and success criteria, individual responses and shared mind approaches all encourage innovation in a fail-safe environment.

Chapter summary

Having read this chapter you will:

- have considered the benefits of open-ended briefs and of outdoor learning;
- understand how curiosity is interwoven through all stages of the iterative design cycle;
- have a deeper understanding of how personal qualities such as resilience, teamwork, patience and determination are developed through the design and technology process.

CHAPTER 10

HARNESSING CURIOSITY ACROSS A WHOLE SCHOOL

Chapter objectives

After reading this chapter you will:

- understand how you might harness curiosity across a whole school;
- be excited about and know how to draw on different primary STEM subjects within one context;
- know how motivating curiosity is for learning.

Overview

This chapter focuses on two schools that have used curiosity to inspire, motivate and teach learners in a different way. School A, which this chapter focuses mainly on, utilises three different strands to achieve high levels of curious children while School B shares many similarities in approach too.

School A: Chapel Break Infant School, Norwich, Norfolk

Chapel Break Infant School (www.chapelbreakinfant.norfolk.sch. uk) is a two form entry school which is situated on the edge of the City of Norwich in Norfolk. For over ten years it has used the teaching of philosophy as a platform of enquiry, encouraging learners to ask deep, philosophical questions such as 'Do dragons exist?' or 'What is it to be human?' The teachers organise the learners' experience around three strands. Strand one is the curriculum, strand two the learning environment and strand three is the Tardis. Curious? Read on!

Strand one – the curriculum

When the English National Curriculum (DfE, 2013) was rewritten the school saw an opportunity to create an exciting new school curriculum that used the content from the National Curriculum (DfE, 2013) but extended it in a way that suited the pupils at their school. The Chapel Break Curiosity Curriculum was born.

The rainbow in Figure 10.1 offers a visual way to understand how the curriculum is arranged. The first band, called *Fact Finders,* represents the content from the National Curriculum (DfE, 2013). The next three bands show how the content sits alongside big ideas, literature, real-life mathematics and many more aspects. Curiosity is an attribute which underpins the whole of this curriculum.

The Chapel Break curriculum is divided into six hives of learning (hives were chosen to tie in with the school's bee logo).

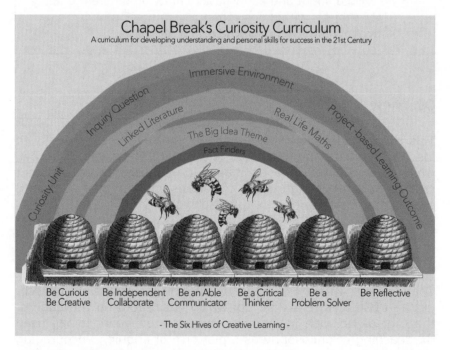

Figure 10.1 The Chapel Break Curiosity Curriculum

The six areas are:

1. be curious, be creative;
2. be independent, collaborate;
3. be an able communicator;
4. be a critical thinker;
5. be a problem solver;
6. be reflective.

The teachers plan using these six areas as the focus of the skills the children are taught, adding in content from the different primary subjects. Since creating their curriculum, the six areas have been remodelled to help the children know which area they are working on while they are learning. During a recent visit to the school, all children aged four upwards were able to say which bee (skill) they were good at, and which they needed to work harder at.

- Be curious, be creative = Wonder bee.
- Be independent, collaborate = Zip twins bees.
- Be an able communicator = Buzz bee.
- Be a critical thinker = Brains bee.
- Be a problem solver = Puzzler bee.
- Be reflective = Austin bee.

Each class has even designed their own models of the bees to help them remember. Can you guess which bees are represented in Figure 10.2?

In some classes the children are also encouraged to keep a record of which bee they have been using as a tally chart (Figure 10.3).

Strand two – the learning environment

The curriculum is only one part of how the school delivers outstanding teaching and learning and is not the only driver in cultivating curiosity. The children at Chapel Break are engaged and stimulated through highly stimulating immersive learning environments. While the school has always sought to use hooks into real world learning, the immersive learning approach is an innovative pedagogical approach. Chapel Break has been using this particular approach since 2014. Like any approach there are principles and values, and the main ones are summarised here:

- Immersive learning environments.
- Project-based learning.
- Challenge-based learning.
- The use of rubrics to support self- and peer assessment.
- Presentation of learning to parents.

Once a term every year group decides on a project or theme, which is presented to the children as a question. Recent questions have included:

- Is ice nice?
- How can we quench the thirst of Africa?
- How can we treat our countryside with care?

Figure 10.2   Four examples of the curriculum bees at Chapel Break Infant School

Figure 10.3 Children keep a tally chart of which bee they are using

These questions offer their own curiosity in the work that follows, but often the learner's initial reaction is to the appearance of the classroom. Over the holidays staff prepare the environment to match the project. So, if the project is about castles, then all tables and chairs are removed, a banqueting table is acquired, along with candelabras, brick wallpaper and a fireplace (see Chapter 2). As the weeks pass the environment is added to actively involve the learners in building their working space. While discrete subjects are still taught, lessons often focus on miniature projects. One task that Year 2 learners were set was to make a digital poster to inform somebody about an African animal. Learners were given free choice as to the animal they chose, but the use of a rubric (a self-assessment tool with different levels of success) sets three levels of challenge, which include to work as a group, to use the Ipad© to find out information

Figure 10.4 Two very proud Year 2 learners

and record a number of suitable facts. In this task learners draw on skills and knowledge from all four primary STEM subjects while their curiosity deepens and keeps them immersed in their work.

> STEM links to science, mathematics, computing and design and technology

Science – to identify and name a variety of animals in their habitats.

Mathematics – to read and write numbers to at least 100.

Design and technology – to generate, develop, model and communicate ideas through drawing templates.

Computing – to use technology purposefully to retrieve digital information.

The two learners in Figure 10.4 were very keen to share their success with their work so far.

Strand three – TARDIS

However, there is one final strand which Chapel Break uses to promote curiosity across the primary STEM subjects, which is the TARDIS. This is both a physical space (a free-standing classroom on the edge of the playground) and a pedagogical approach. It stands for the Thinking Artistic Reflective Dialogue Imagination Studio. Established in 1998 the purpose of the TARDIS is to allow learners to explore, create and collaborate in activities that are designed specifically to make them think and be curious. Learners of all year groups spend up to three days at a time, twice a year in the TARDIS. The initial stage is spent on the 'thinking side' of the studio from which a story book, piece of artwork, short film or an experience is used to open an enquiry. Skills such as listening, thinking, taking turns, communicating, reasoning, justifying, debating and critique are just a few examples of what might be built upon and taken back into the classroom. Ideas are generated and constructed by the learners, promoting creativity, curiosity and deeper level thinking. Learners' ideas are drawn upon in the 'messy side' of the studio from which they are able to explore and experiment with drawing, painting, sculpting, print making and mixed-media outcomes. Artwork is exhibited around the school and also in an annual show at the Norwich Arts Centre and as part of the Norfolk and Norwich Festival Open Studios, all of which are open to public viewing.

The TARDIS is currently run by Jennie Walker, who trained in art and design, teaching first in secondary schools before moving to Chapel Break Infant School. Jennie has selected four case studies to share in this chapter. All four use curiosity as a way to engage learners but they also draw on the skills and content knowledge from across all the primary STEM subjects.

CASE STUDY

Henry Moore

Science – identifying, naming and comparing a variety of materials based on their physical properties

Mathematics – exploring 2D and 3D shapes

Computing – using technology purposefully to digitally record observations (using photographs)

Design and Technology – designing, making, evaluating and critiquing work while building up technical knowledge

STEM links to science, mathematics, computing and design and technology

Henry Moore was an English sculptor and artist who is best known for his bronze sculptures of the human figure. To launch this project Year 2 children visited the Sainsbury's Centre for Visual Arts (SCVA), situated

(Continued)

(Continued)

in the grounds of the University of East Anglia, Norwich (www.scva. ac.uk) which houses a display of Moore's sculptures, letters and art work (Figure 10.5).

Learners talked about the importance of statues: what makes them important? Why are they significant? The material, scale, value? In particular, learners focused on the sculptures, asking questions such as 'Why are mothers so important?' The children then spent time drawing a large-scale sculpture, looking closely at proportion, scale and texture. They took photographs of their favourite sculptures to help them remember when they were back in the classroom.

Figure 10.5 Learners sketching outside the SCVA

Back in school within the TARDIS learners looked carefully at how to transfer 2D drawings into 3D models using wire, sticks and Polystyrene©. They then covered them with Mod-Roc©, waiting for it to dry before applying black tissue paper with wax crayon to complete the sculpture (Figure 10.6).

Figure 10.6   Two three-dimensional models in the style of Henry Moore

Finally, learners critiqued their own work and one another's. They revisited the original question and the children made constructive, positive and helpful comments about the sculptures. At each step of the journey learners' interest and curiosity is sparked. However, it is also interesting to see how the four primary STEM subjects play their own part in this journey too. Often we use skills and knowledge from other subjects but the links are implicit. Perhaps we need to make these links more explicit to learners so they can see how their mathematical or computing skills are helping them to make unique sculptures in the style of Henry Moore.

CASE STUDY

What is beautiful?

Science – observing and describing weather and seasonal changes in the world

Mathematics – looking at the properties and position and direction of shapes

Design and Technology – generating, developing, modeling and communicating their ideas through talking and drawing

Computing – using technology purposefully (to access a YouTube film)

(Continued)

STEM links to science, mathematics, computing and design and technology

(Continued)

The Reception class had chosen Antarctica as their termly project and so the work in the TARDIS focused on looking at this landscape, colours, contours and animals from an aesthetic point of view using images like the one in Figure 10.7. Curiosity was evoked by showing learners a short YouTube film (www.youtube.com/watch?v=sIujRh4g6lw) of an expedition to the Antarctic, looking at its wondrous beauty.

Figure 10.7 Photograph of an iceberg

Learners were then asked, 'What is beautiful?' While learners initially began to name people (e.g. their mother), feelings and emotions towards a person soon became more prolific and important than the actual appearance of a person. They looked at the work of John Virtue (a local artist) and watched demonstrations on how to use and move monochrome paint to represent beautiful wave actions of the sea (Figure 10.8). In groups of five they then created amazing, thought-provoking images.

Figure 10.8   Curiosity inspired through film and exhibited through paint

CASE STUDY

What it means to be different

Science – identify, name, draw and label some of the basic parts of the human body (animals, including humans)

Mathematics – using reasoning and problem-solving skills to fit together shapes and lines

(Continued)

STEM links to science, mathematics, computing and design and technology

(Continued)

Design and Technology – making and evaluating (cutting and shaping, exploring and evaluating a range of products)

Computing – using technology purposefully (to look at the artwork of Magritte and Hoch)

The stimulus for this project came from the artist René Magritte:

- *Le Blanc Seing*, René Magritte, 1965
- *The Empire of Light*, René Magritte, 1950
- *Not to be Reproduced*, René Magritte, 1937
- *The Future of Statues*, René Magritte, 1937

Year 2 learners discussed what the word 'surrealism' meant, which developed into the question 'What does it mean to be different?' Learners debated the question, outlining their own opinions on whether different was good, bad or both. They talked about why we need to be different and why we want things to be different. Learners gave reasons and justifications.

They then looked at the work of Hannah Hoch and thought about changing faces. A portrait photograph was taken of each child and having sourced facial features from magazines, learners re-created the work of Hannah Hoch using their own faces. They transformed themselves into surrealist images. Using materials they found, learners then created surrealist backgrounds for their portraits, sketching out dreamlike landscapes. The final outcomes were thought provoking, surreal and a little bit frightening.

Figure 10.9   Two images of surrealism used as a basis for stimulating curiosity

Following a critique, learners became more comfortable with the concept of 'different being okay'. The more surreal their artwork was, the more proud they were (Figure 10.9). They demonstrated confidence in understanding the word 'surrealism' and expressed differences between one another and in themselves as positive attitudes.

CASE STUDY

Memories

Science – understanding human characteristics (animals, including humans).

Mathematics – recognising, naming and using 2D and 3D shapes.

Design and Technology – generate, develop, model and communicate their ideas through talking and drawing.

Computing – using technology purposefully (to look at the artwork of Marshe).

STEM links to science, mathematics, computing and design and technology

The big question for this group was *How do we choose our pathways in life?* After reading the book *The Paper Dolls* (Donaldson, 2013) the group led the philosophical enquiry towards their own memories and the group decision to take forward the question *Can we choose the memories we keep?* was agreed. Learners looked at some of the artwork of Jivya Marshe who was a member of the Warli tribe. The tribe's methods use very simple forms to make art, depicting hunting, dancing, sowing and harvesting. As a child, Marshe communicated only by using drawings in the dust of circles, squares and triangles.

Each child printed on to paper dolls and then constructed a collaborative piece of art by making a giant swirl on canvas (Figure 10.10). Natural Indian pigments were used on the background of the canvas and a variety of squares, circles and triangles were cut out and carefully placed on it.

(Continued)

(Continued)

Figure 10.10   A curious and collaborative piece of art work by Year 1 learners

All four case studies above evoked learners' curiosity using different starting points, while also drawing on different STEM subjects.

School B: Hevingham Primary School, Hevingham, Norfolk

Hevingham Primary School (www.hevinghamprimary.co.uk) is a small village school situated north of the City of Norwich in Norfolk. It has adopted a more contextual approach for some of its teaching. It still values the importance of discrete subjects but also recognises the value of making connections across subjects.

CASE STUDY

Living in space

Science – working scientifically, forces and magnets, everyday materials, Earth and space.

Mathematics – solving problems, reasoning, presenting data in a variety of ways.

Design and Technology – designing, making, evaluating, using technical knowledge.

Computing – using technology purposefully.

> STEM links to science, mathematics, computing and design and technology

This context was inspired by the story (15 December 2015) that the UK astronaut Major Tim Peake was to go to and live on the international space station for six months. This offered learners at Hevingham Primary School the opportunity to think about the science of living in space (Figure 10.11). This is not the same as living on Earth.

A series of activities were set up for learners to investigate and think about which Tim and the crew had demonstrated on the Space Station. One activity asked learners to fill a plastic bag three-quarters full with

Figure 10.11   Learners watch a live broadcast from the International Space Station

(Continued)

(Continued)

water and then push a pencil through the bag and observe what happens (Figure 10.12). Does the bag leak water? If you want to try this experiment yourself, make sure the pencils are sharp to make it easy to push them into the bag (but do not push the pencil all the way through!). The temperature of the water does not affect the outcome.

Look away now if you don't want to know the answer! The reason the bag does not leak is because plastic bags are made from polymers. Polymers are long chains of individual molecules, called monomers. When the plastic bag is punctured the pencil is separating the polymer chain without breaking it. The molecules then squeeze in tight around the pencil to prevent any leak occurring. However, once the pencil is removed the bag will leak!

Figure 10.12 Learners puncture a plastic bag with a pencil, but will the bag leak?

In another activity learners were given two magnets and asked to generate their own questions from this simple starting point. Some learners tested the attraction and repulsion of magnets, while others tested materials with magnets (Figure 10.13).

After learners had completed the activities they were asked, 'Where is the science?' This provoked even more discussion and fuelled learners' curiosity further by linking what they *had* learned into what they *could* learn next.

Using a context such as *Living in Space* allows learners to use a range of skills and knowledge from different subjects in a short space of time. They are not told that the next hour will be dedicated to mathematics or science. They do not use the clues of being in the computer suite to realise that the next phase of learning will centre on computing skills. While it is important to maintain discrete time to teach subjects in isolation, it is easy to see how a context can spark curiosity as well as practising different skills at once.

Figure 10.13   One learner tests to see if his finger is attracted or repulsed by a magnet

Conclusion

This book began by presenting different definitions of curiosity, along with a rationale as to why it is an essential attribute in primary classrooms. It has ended with examples from two schools which are deliberately cultivating curiosity. While we have shown throughout each chapter that curiosity can be self-initiated and pursued, learners often need a catalyst to stimulate it. Building on the previous eight chapters, Chapter 10 offers different ways of harnessing all primary STEM subjects together through activities that are tried and tested to spark curious learners who want to engage in learning and be successful in it. If you value curiosity you already have the qualities needed to foster this in your learners. Why not make curiosity a key focus of your classroom, curriculum and teaching so that your learners benefit from its potential to inspire, challenge and motivate?

Chapter summary

Having read this chapter you will:

- have a clear understanding of how curiosity can be created and captured through a variety of mediums;
- see opportunities of how to link the four primary STEM subjects together in one activity;
- have had the opportunity to see how two schools have tailored and organised their curriculum to inspire learners.

REFERENCES AND BIBLIOGRAPHY

Alexander, R. (2010) *Children, their World, Their Education: Final report and recommendations of the Cambridge Primary Review*, London: Routledge.

America Press Institute (2015) *How millennials use and control social media*. Accessed at: www.americanpressinstitute.org/publications/reports/survey-research/millennials-social-media/ on 22.02.16

Argyris, C.S. and Schön, D. (1978) *Organisational Learning: A theory of action and perspective.* Reading: Adison-Wesley.

Aronoff, J. (1962) Freud's conception of the origin of curiosity. *Journal of Psychology*, 54, pp. 39–45.

Askew, M., Brown, M., Rhodes, V., Johnson, D. and Wiliam, D. (1997) *Effective Teachers of Numeracy*. Final Report. London: King's College.

Athey, C. (2007) *Extending Thought in Young Children: A parent–teacher partnership*. London: SAGE.

Bagge, P. (2015) *Code-IT Primary Programming: How to teach primary programming using Scratch*. Buckingham: University of Buckingham Press.

Barnes, J. (2011) *Cross-Curricular Learning* (2nd edition) London: Sage.

Berlyne, D. E. (1954) A theory of human curiosity. *British Journal of Psychology* 45 (3), pp. 180–191.

Berry, M. (2013a) *Computing in the National Curriculum: A guide for primary teachers*. Accessed at: www.computingatschool.org.uk/data/uploads/CASPrimaryComputing.pdf on 22.02.16

Berry, M. (2013b) *Computing: It's not just what we teach but how we teach it*. Switched On – Computing at School Newsletter. Accessed at: www.computingatschool.org.uk/data/uploads/newsletter-autumn-2013.pdf on 23.02.16

Bibby, T. (2002) Shame: an emotional response to doing mathematics as an adult and a teacher. *British Educational Research Journal*, 28 (5), pp. 705–721.

Boaler, J. (2016) *Mathematical Mindsets*. San Francisco, CA: Jossey-Bass.

Boaler, J. (2014) *Changing the Conversation about Girls and STEM.* Washington, DC: The White House. Accessed at: www.youcubed. org on 12.12.15

Body, W. (1999) *Anna's Amazing Multi-Coloured Glasses.* Pearson Education.

Borthwick, A. (2008) *Children's Perceptions of and Attitudes Towards Mathematics Lessons in Primary Schools,* unpublished thesis.

Brown, M., Brown, P. and Bibby, T. (2008) 'I would rather die': reasons given by 16-year-olds for not continuing their study of mathematics education. *Research in Mathematics Education,* 10 (1), pp. 3–18.

Bruner, J. S. (1957) *Going Beyond the Information Given.* New York: Norton.

Caro, C. (2012). *Schema's in Children's Play.* Accessed at: www.nature-play.co.uk/blog/schemas-in-childrens-play on 18.02.16

Cherryh, C. J. (1995) *Tripoint.* London: Hodder & Stoughton.

Creighton, C. (1889) *Jenner and Vaccination – A Strange Chapter of Medical History.* London: Swan Sonnenschein & Co.

Cross, A. and Board, J. (2014) *Creative Ways to Teach Primary Science.* Maidenhead: Open University Press/McGraw Hill.

Cross, A. and Borthwick, A. (2016) *Connecting Primary Maths and Science.* London: Open University Press/McGraw Hill.

Cross, A. and Bowden, A. (2014) *Essential Primary Science (2nd Edition)* Maidenhead: Open University Press/McGraw Hill.

Crouch, T. (2002) *First Flight: The Wright Brothers and the invention of the airplane.* U.S. Centennial of Flight Commission, Government Printing Office. Accessed at: www.centennialofflight.net/essay/Wright_Bros/ wright_family/WR1.htm on 08.03.16

Darling-Hammond, L. (2000) Teacher quality and student achievement. *Education Policy Analysis Archives,* 8 (1).

DATA (2013) *Characteristics of a Genuine D&T Experience within the School Curriculum: Principles for guiding and evaluating practice.* Accessed at: www.data.org.uk/media/1130/school-curriculum-princi ples-for-dt.pdf on 10.01.16

DATA (2015) *Primary.* Wellsbourne: The Design Technology Association. Accessed at: www.data.org.uk/for-education/primary/ on 18.02.16

Department for Education (2012) *Development Matters in the Early Years Foundation Stage (EYFS).* Accessed at: www.foundationyears. org.uk/files/2012/03/Development-Matters-FINAL-PRINT-AMENDED. pdf on 18.02.16

Department for Education (2013) *The National Curriculum in England: Key Stage 1 and 2 Framework Document,* London: DfE.

Department for Education (2014) *EYFS Statutory Framework. London: DfE.* Accessed at: www.foundationyears.org.uk/eyfs-statutory-framework/ on 16.02.16

Department for Education (2012) *Teachers' Standards.* London: DfE.

Department for Education and Employment / Qualifications and Curriculum Authority (1999) *The National Curriculum for Key Stages 1 and 2,* London: DfEE/QCA.

Department for Education and Skills (2006) *Learning Outside the Classroom Manifesto.* London: DfES. Accessed at: http://webarchive.

nationalarchives.gov.uk/20130401151715/http://education. gov.uk/ publications/eorderingdownload/lotc.pdf on 09.03.16

Devlin, K. (1997) *Mathematics: The science of patterns: The search for order in life, mind and the universe.* Scientific American Library: New York.

Dewey, J. (1910) *How We Think.* Lexington, MA: Heath.

Donaldson, J. (2013) *The Paper Dolls.* London: Macmillan Publishers.

Duckworth, E. (1972) The having of wonderful ideas. *Harvard Educational Review* 42(2), pp. 217–231.

Dunn, R. (2013) Be curious: Understanding 'curiosity' in contemporary curriculum policy and practice, *Education 3–13*, 41 (6), pp. 557–561 Abingdon: Routledge/Taylor & Francis.

Dweck, C.S. (2006) *Mindset: The New Psychology of Success.* New York: Ballantine Books.

Engel, S. (2015) *The Hungry Mind.* Massachusetts, MA: Harvard University Press.

Flavell, J. (1979) Metacognition and cognitive monitoring: A new area of cognitive-developmental. *American Psychologist*, 34 (10), October, pp. 906–911.

France, A. (1881) *The Crime of Sylvestre Bonnard.* Available at: fr.wikisource. org/wiki/Le_Crime_de_Sylvestre_Bonnard Assessed on 16.02.16

Freud, S. (2015) Analysis of a phobia in a five year old boy in *Collected Papers* (Vol. 3, pp. 149–289). New York: Basic Books.

Gruber, M. J., Gelman, B. D. and Ranganath, C. (2014) States of curiosity modulate hippocampus-dependent learning via the dopaminergic circuit. *Neuron*, 84 (2), pp. 486–496.

Hawkins, D. (2009) *Healing and Recovery.* Sedona: Veritas Publishing.

Haylock, D. (2010) *Mathematics Explained for Primary Teachers.* London: SAGE.

Hopkins, D. R. (2002) *The Greatest Killer: Smallpox in History.* Chicago: University of Chicago Press.

Jobs, S. (1996) *Steve Jobs: The next insanely great thing. Wired* (on line magazine): Redwood City. Accessed at: www.wired.com/ 1996/02/jobs-2/ on 16.02.16

Jones, R. W. (2004) *Creativity in the Primary Classroom.* London: Routledge.

Kimbell, R., Stables, K., Wheeler, T., Wozniak, A. and Kelly, V. (1991) *The Assessment of Performance in Design and Technology: The final Report of the Design and Technology APU Project.* London: Schools Examination and Assessment Authority.

Leavitt, D. (2007) *The Man Who Knew Too Much: Alan Turing and the invention of computers.* London: Orion Publishing.

Lieberman, J. N. (2014) *Playfulness: Its relationship to imagination and creativity.* Academic Press.

Litman, J. A. (2005) Curiosity and the pleasures of learning: Wanting and liking new information *Cognition and Emotion* 19 (6), pp. 793–814.

Livingstone, I. and Hope, A. (2011) *Next Gen. Transforming the UK into the world's leading talent hub for the video games and visual effects industries*. Accessed at: www.nesta.org.uk/sites/default/files/next_gen_wv.pdf on 22.02.16

Loewenstein, G. (1994) The psychology of curiosity: A review and reinterpretation. *Psychological Bulletin*, 116 (1), pp. 75–98.

Mason, J., Graham, A. and Johnston-Wilder, S. (2005) *Developing Thinking in Algebra*. London: Paul Chapman Publishing.

Mason, J. and Johnston-Wilder, S. (2004) *Fundamental Constructs in Mathematics Education*. London: Routledge/Falmer.

McClure, L. (2011) *Using Low Threshold High Ceiling Tasks in Ordinary Classrooms*. Published September, July. Accessed: 02.01.16 www.nrich.maths.org

McLeod, S. (2008) *Bruner*. Accessed at: www.simplypsychology.org/bruner.html on 16.02.16

McLeod, S. (2015) *Jean Piaget*. Accessed at: www.simplypsychology.org/piaget.html#schema on 16.02.16

Mental Health Foundation (2015) *Children and Young People*. Accessed at www.mentalhealth.org.uk: www.mentalhealth.org.uk/a-to-z/c/children-and-young-people on 17.02.16

Monica, P. (2015) *Facebook now worth more than Walmart.* Accessed at: http://money.cnn.com/2015/06/23/investing/facebook-walmart-market-value/ on 22.02.16

Moser, J., Schroder, H. S., Heeter, C., Moran, T. P. and Lee, Y. H. (2011) Mind your errors: Evidence for a neural mechanism linking growth mindset to adaptive post error adjustments. *Psychological Science,* 22, pp. 1484–1489.

Mulholland, N. (ed.) (2006) *The Psychology of Harry Potter: An unauthorized examination of the boy who lived.* Dallas, TX: BenBella Books.

Nardi, E. and Steward, S. (2003) Is mathematics T.I.R.E.D.? A profile of quiet disaffection in the secondary mathematics classroom. *British Educational Research Journal*, 29 (3), pp. 345–367.

Naylor, S. and Keogh, B. (2000) *Concept Cartoons in Science Education*. Sandbach: Millgate House Publishers.

Newton, D. (2005) *Teaching Design and Technology*, 5–11. London: Paul Chapman Publishing.

Ofsted (2008) *Learning Outside the Classroom: How Far Should You Go?* Accessed at: www.leics.gov.uk/learning_outside_the_classroom.pdf on 17.02.16.

Ofsted (2013) *Maintaining Curiosity: A survey into science education in schools*. Manchester: Office for Standards in Education.

Ofsted (2013a) *Design and Technology Professional Development Materials for Primary Schools*. Accessed at: www.slideshare.net/Ofstednews/design-and-technology-professional-development-materials-for-primary-schools on 16.0216

Outterside, Y. (1993) The emergence of design ability: the Early Years. *IDATER Conference*. Loughborough: IDATER.

Papert, S. (1993) *Mindstorms: Children, computers and powerful ideas (2nd edition)*. New York: Basic Books.

Piaget, J. (1952) *The Origins of Intelligence in Children*. New York: International University Press.

Piaget, J. (1958) *The Child's Construction of Reality*. London: Routledge & Kegan Paul.

Piaget, J. (1969) *Psychology of Intelligence.* New York: Littlefield Adams.

Piggott, J. and Back, J. (2011) *A Problem is Only a Problem When You Can't Do It*. Accessed at: www.nrich.maths.org on 9.02.16

Polya, G. (1945) *How to Solve it*. Princeton, NJ: Princeton University Press.

Program for International Student Assessment (PISA) (2012) *PISA 2012 results in focus: What 15-year olds know and what they can do with what they know*. Paris: OECD.

Quinn, S. (1995) *Marie Curie: A Life*. London: Mandarin.

Redmund, C. (2005) The Creativity Wheel: Assessing creative development. London: Creative Partnerships.

Resnick, M. and Rosenbaum, E. (2013). Designing for tinkerability in M. Honey and D. Kanter (eds) *Design, Make, Play: Growing the Next Generation of STEM Innovators*. London: Routledge.

Rose, J. (2009) *Independent Review of the Primary Curriculum*: Final Report, London: DCSF.

Rowling, J. (2003) *Harry Potter and the Order of the Phoenix*. London: Bloomsbury.

Royal Society (2012) *Shut down or restart? The way forward for computing in UK schools*. Accessed at: https://royalsociety.org/~/media/education/computing-in-schools/2012-01-12-computing-in-schools.pdf on 23.02.16

Royal Society (2014) *Vision for Science and Mathematics Education*. London: The Royal Society.

Rushkoff, D. (2011) *Program or be Programmed: 10 commandments for a digital age*. New York: Soft Skull Press.

Russell, S. J. (2000) Developing computational fluency with whole numbers in the elementary grades, in B. J. Ferrucci and K. M. Heid (eds) Millennium Focus Issue: Perspectives on Principles and Standards, *New England Maths Journal*, XXXII (2), pp. 40–54.

Schmidt, W. H., McKnight, C. C., Cogan, L. S., Jakwerth, P. M., Houang, R. T., Wiley, D. E. and Raizen, S. A. (2002) *Facing the Consequences: Using TIMSS for a closer look at US mathematics and science education*. Dordrecht: Kluwer Academic Publishers.

Schulman. L. S. (1986) Those who understand: A conception of teacher knowledge. *Educational Researcher*, February., pp.4–14.

Senechal, M. (1990) *On the Shoulders of Giants: New Approaches to Numeracy*. Lynn Arthur Steen (ed.) Washington, DC: National Academy Press, pp. 139–181.

Sharples, M. A. (2013) *Innovating Pedagogy 2013: Open University Innovation Report 2*. Accessed at: www.open.ac.uk/iet/main/sites/www.open.ac.uk.iet.main/files/files/ecms/web-content/Innovating_Pedagogy_report_2013.pdf on 19.02.16

Sharples, M. A. et al. (2013) *Innovating Pedagogy 2014: Open University Innovation Report 3*. Accessed at: www.openuniversity.edu/sites/www.openuniversity.edu/files/The_Open_University_Innovating_Pedagogy_2014_0.pdf on 16.02.16

Skemp, R. (1976) Relational understanding and instrumental under-
standing. *Mathematical Teaching*, 77, pp. 20–26.
Smale, W. (2004) *Profile: The Google Founders*. Accessed at: http://
news.bbc.co.uk/1/hi/business/3666241.stm on 23.02.16
Solomon, J. (1993) *Teaching Science, Technology and Society*, London:
Open University Press.
Swade, D. (2001) *The Cogwheel Brain: Charles Babbage and the quest
to build the first computer*. London: Abacus.
Swan, M. (2005) *Improving Learning in Mathematics: Challenges and
Strategies*. London: Department for Education and Skills Standard
Unit.
Tabak, A. (2004) *Hundreds register for new Facebook website*. Accessed at:
www.thecrimson.com/article/2004/2/9/hundreds-register-for-new-
facebook-website/on 23.02.16
Turing, A.M. (1950) Computing, Machinery and Intelligence. *Mind* (59),
pp. 433–460
Turner, J. et al. (2013) *It's not fair – or is it? A guide to developing
children's ideas through primary science enquiry*. Sandbach: Millgate
House Publishing.
U.S. Department of Defense, 2002. DoD News Briefing – Secretary
Rumsfeld and Gen. Myers. Accessed at: http://archive.defense.gov/
Transcripts/Transcript.aspx?TranscriptID=2636 on 28.01.16
Vygotsky, L. (1978) Interaction between learning and development.
Mind and Society, 79–91. Cambridge, MA: Harvard University Press.

INDEX

Added to a page number 'f' denotes a figure.